"The Telling"
Christ in the Passover
Warren Chaney, Ph.D.

WESTBOW
PRESS®
A DIVISION OF THOMAS NELSON
& ZONDERVAN

Scripture quotations taken from the New American Standard Bible®, Copyright © 1960, 1962, 1963, 1968, 1971, 1972, 1973, 1975, 1977, 1995 by The Lockman Foundation Used by permission." (www.Lockman.org)

WestBow Press books may be ordered through booksellers or by contacting:

WestBow Press
A Division of Thomas Nelson & Zondervan
1663 Liberty Drive
Bloomington, IN 47403
www.westbowpress.com
1 (866) 928-1240

ISBN: 978-1-9736-6046-0 (sc)
ISBN: 978-1-9736-6045-3 (hc)
ISBN: 978-1-9736-6047-7 (e)

Library of Congress Control Number: 2019904636

Print information available on the last page.

WestBow Press rev. date: 07/30/2019

DEDICATION

This book is dedicated to my parents *(Herbert & Izetta Chaney),* and to my grandparents *(Smith & Rollie Chaney* and *Cleve & Ora Farmer).* They are gone now, but their legacy remains, as a positive influence on their children, and their children's children. Parenting is the most important job that the Lord gives us and they did it well. I pray that this book reflects a fraction of the effort that they put into their offspring and grandchildren.

ACKNOWLEDGMENT

My thanks to those who helped me stage the many Passover services over the past decades. Without them, this book would not have been written. I am especially grateful to my dear friend, Carl McPherson, who, many years ago, started me on this journey. Thanks also to my close ally, Steve McConkey, who supported the development of this book and knew that I would write it, even before I did.

Leanne Brasington, Anne Rose, and Deb McConkey were the book's editors, and I cannot express enough, my eternal gratitude for the job that they did. Editing is one of the toughest and perhaps most unrewarding jobs in writing. Their dedication to their craft made this a much better book than it would otherwise have been.

Nothing happens without the Lord and I am especially grateful for the opportunity He has given me along with the time to develop and write this story of the Lord's Passover.

TABLE OF CONTENTS

FOREWORD

I have had the good fortune to conduct many Christian Passovers over the past decades. When I first began, few Christians were interested. Since then, I have seen the Christian Passover grow from an isolated event here and there to a worldwide explosion of interest throughout our Churches. When I first researched background material, it was quite sparse with few books on the subject. This was stunning in light of the affirmation of our faith that is so present in Passover. Therefore, I resolved to one-day write a book on how a church or family may conduct such a service as outreach and/or teaching tool. Fortunately, I did not write one earlier, because I lacked the understanding to do so.

As time passed, the experience I received from conducting and observing numerous Passovers convinced me that a thorough book on "how to do one" needed to be written along with an explanation of who to do one in your home.

The book that I have written turns out to be larger and more expansive than I envisioned and I ended up writing two smaller books (*A Christian Haggadah* and *A Leader's Guide*) as accompaniments or accessories to this book. You will not need the latter two to use this book, but if you decide to conduct your own Passover, they will be helpful.

Conducting a Christian Passover Seder is a blessing. It's a blessing for those who do it and for those who attend. For some of you, this may become an outreach ministry. If the LORD moves even one person who reads this book, then I feel my efforts in writing this are justified.

May GOD, bless you in your endeavors and may you receive a blessing from the contents of this volume and from the Passover services that you conduct.

THE PROPHECY OF CHRIST IN PASSOVER

CHAPTER 1
THE PROPHECY OF CHRIST IN PASSOVER

'...In the first month, on the fourteenth day of the month at twilight is the LORD's Passover. 'Then on the fifteenth day of the same month there is the Feast of Unleavened Bread to the LORD; for seven days you shall eat unleavened bread....'
Leviticus 23:5-6

The Apostle Paul points out in the New Testament that the Jewish Holy Days—the feasts and celebrations—were a shadow of the things to come through Jesus the Messiah.[1] Although "believers" haven't traditionally celebrated the holidays in a biblical sense, there is a robust Christian significance within each of the Holy Days, especially the first one, Passover. Although we may choose not to commemorate these holidays, as we discover the importance of each, we will gain a better knowledge of God's Word, an improved understanding of the Bible, and a deeper relationship with the Lord.

Jesus and the Events Before Passover

Three of the Lord's feast days play a vital role in the crucifixion and resurrection of Jesus. The feasts of Passover, Firstfruits, and Unleavened Bread fall within a consecutive eight-day period.[2] This entire period is known as both the Passover Feast and the Feast of Unleavened Bread, as prescribed by the laws of the original Sinai Covenant.[3] The offering of animals in memorial of the first Passover in Egypt was to take place on the 14th of Nisan, and the eating of the

---

[1] Colossians 2:16-17
[2] Exodus 12:6; Leviticus 23:5; Numbers 9:1-2, 28:16; Leviticus 23:9-14.
[3] Leviticus 23

sacrifice by the community in their homes on the 15th of Nisan, the night of the full moon for that calendar month.

Six days before Passover, Jesus had traveled to Bethany, where Lazarus lived, and dinner was provided in Jesus' honor. At this meal, Mary took nearly a pint of pure nard, an expensive perfume worth about a year's wages, poured it on Jesus' feet, and wiped his feet with her hair. According to John 12, Judas Iscariot, one of Jesus' disciples, vehemently objected, asking, *"Why was this perfume not sold for three hundred denarii and given to poor people?"*

The gospels tell us that others attending the dinner also objected, but Jesus replied, *"Let her alone, so that she may keep it for the day of My burial* [8] *"For you always have the poor with you, but you do not always have Me."* [4] Thus, in the week of Passover, the biblical symbolism concerning what was to transpire became increasingly pronounced.

There appear to be two meals discussed in some of the gospels. The main scriptural point supporting two dinners is that Judas was unable to betray Jesus and set the events of His arrest and crucifixion in motion until Christ's "time" had arrived. There is no reference to Judas' treachery in the events before or after the feast mentioned in John 12:1-11. Jesus' "hour" in John's Gospel doesn't transpire until John 13:1.

The Bible records that Jesus left Bethany six days before Passover. From there, He sent two disciples into the village to secure a donkey that had been tied there but never ridden. Christ rode this donkey into Jerusalem on Palm Sunday. It is on this day that Christ fulfilled the Old Testament prophecies of Genesis 49:10-12, [10] *"The scepter shall not depart from Judah, Nor the ruler's staff from between his feet, Until Shiloh comes, And to him shall be the obedience of the peoples.* [11]

---

[4] John 12:5, 7, 8

"He ties his foal to the vine, And his donkey's colt to the choice vine; He washes his garments in wine, And his robes in the blood of grapes. [12] *"His eyes are dull from wine, And his teeth white from milk...."*

The Jews were also aware of the Zechariah 9:9 prophecy, [9] *"Rejoice greatly, O daughter of Zion! Shout in triumph, O daughter of Jerusalem! Behold, your king is coming to you; He is just and endowed with salvation, Humble, and mounted on a donkey, Even on a colt, the foal of a donkey."*

Those witnessing the Galilean's ride into Jerusalem saw this as the coronation day discussed in 1 Kings 1:33-35: [33]*And the king said to them, "Take with you the servants of your lord, and have my son Solomon ride on my own mule, and bring him down to Gihon.* [34]*And let Zadok the priest and Nathan the prophet anoint him there as king over Israel, and blow the trumpet and say, 'Long live King Solomon!'* [35]*Then you shall come up after him, and he shall come and sit on my throne and be king in my place; for I have appointed him to be ruler over Israel and Judah."*

As Jesus approached Jerusalem, He looked at the city and wept over it, foretelling the suffering that awaited the city. The gospels recount how, as Jesus rode, the people laid their cloaks and small branches of trees in front of him. It is important to note that palm branches were used to welcome great conquerors.[5]

The fulfillment of Zechariah's Messianic prophecy together with the other prophecies of Isaiah connected the Messiah to King David's line and joined with the visual image recalling Solomon's triumphant ride. This encouraged the multitudes to cry out just as their ancestors had, *"...Hosanna! Blessed is He who comes in the Name of the Lord, even the King of Israel."*[6]

---

[5] 1 Maccabees 13:51; 2 Maccabees 10:7
[6] John 12:13

The Hebrew word *Hosanna* means "O Lord, grant salvation." "He who comes in the name of the Lord" is referenced in Psalm 118:26, but here it is a title for Jesus, the King of Israel, given in connection with the quotation from Zechariah 9:9.

Considering the adoration and praise heaped on Jesus, it is of little wonder that when the temple authorities heard even the children shouting, *"Hosanna to the Son of David,"* [7] in the temple, they became irate. When the chief priests and scribes saw Him overturn the temple trading tables, teach the crowds in parables directed at the leaders, and perform miraculous healings, they were angry, indignant, and threatened. They wanted him dead and began immediately to look for a way to accomplish that end. The leaders plotted to kill Jesus in a way that would not attract the attention of the vast multitudes that followed him. The scribes, Pharisees, and others were afraid to take him while the crowds were watching. Luke 22 explains that Satan was on the move and entered into Judas, leading him to discuss with the chief priests and officers of the temple how he might betray Jesus. [8]

Jesus Celebrates the Passover—Symbolism, and Meaning

Christ celebrated Passover. The scriptures tell us that Jesus was eager to share the Seder [pronounced "say-der"] meal with the disciples. Jesus gave Peter and John these instructions: *"...[W]hen you have entered the city, a man will meet you carrying a pitcher of water; follow him into the house that he enters. And you shall say to the owner of the house, 'The Teacher says to you,*

---

[7] Matthew 21:15
[8] Luke 22:3-5

"Where is the guest room in which I may eat the Passover with My disciples?"...[9]

The owner provided the disciples with a large furnished upper room. There the disciples personally prepared the Passover. John illustrates that this the time when Jesus fulfilled the prophecy that, "His hour had come."[10]

When the time for Passover arrived, Jesus and his disciples reclined at the table already set for them. *And He said to them, "I have earnestly desired to eat this Passover with you before I suffer: for I say to you, I shall never again eat it until it is fulfilled in the kingdom of God."*[11]

During the Seder meal, while the disciples were eating, Jesus told them, *"Truly I say to you that one of you will betray Me."*[12] This proclamation upset the disciples, and they began questioning who it would be, each declaring he was not the one.

Christ answered the questions by saying, *"He who dipped his hand with Me in the bowl is the one who will betray Me."*[13] What is significant is that "the dipping of the bread" into the bowl was part of the Passover ceremony that occurs when a *Korech* or *matzah* (unleavened bread) dipped in bitter herbs is prepared and eaten. This "sop," correctly identified in John 13:26 KJV by the Apostle John, was eaten with lamb during the temple era in Jerusalem. As in the past and as is still the custom today; one gives a sop dipped in the bitter herbs to a loved one at the table. That Jesus gave His sop to one who would shortly sell Him out to the authorities is spellbinding. In that moment of personal pain, Jesus was telling Judas that He loved him.

---

[9] Luke 22:10-11
[10] John 13:1
[11] Luke 22:15-16
[12] Matthew 26:20-22
[13] Matthew 26:23

Immediately after Jesus dipped the sop and gave it to Judas, Judas left to betray Him.[14]

Later as they were eating, Jesus took the bread, gave thanks, broke it and gave it to them, saying, *"This is My body which is given for you; do this in remembrance of Me."*[15] Afterward, He took a cup, gave thanks and said, *"Drink from it, all of you; for this is My blood of the covenant, which is to be shed on behalf of many for the forgiveness of sins...."*

Then Jesus declared, *"But I say to you, I will not drink of this fruit of the vine from now on until that day when I drink it new with you in My Father's kingdom."*[16]

Most Christians understand and have heard the words addressed to the disciples during the breaking of the bread and drinking of the wine. Many are unaware of how Jesus' actions fit into specific parts of the Passover Seder and consequently have a more significant meaning than can be conveyed during a traditional communion service.

The beauty of the Messianic Passover is that it tells us what Jesus' Last Supper was like. The Seder explains the historical significance of the elements used for 2,000 years of Holy Communion. No amount of reading, teaching, or explaining can replace witnessing and taking part in such a Passover.

> **Passover cannot be seen. It must be experienced!**

The Cup and Breaking of Bread

Jews historically drink four cups of wine at the Seder. The third cup called the "cup of blessing" or "cup of redemption," is the specific cup upon which communion is based. Paul spoke of this in 1 Corinthians 10:16: *Is not*

---

[14] John 13:26-30
[15] Luke 22:19
[16] Matthew 26:27-29

the cup of blessing which we bless a sharing in the blood of Christ?

God the Trinity – Father, Son, and Holy Spirit

The bread from the Last Supper is the *Afikomen* of the Passover Seder. It is the middle of three pieces of matzah on the Passover table. The most common utterance of faith in Judaism is taken from Deuteronomy 6:4, which reads, *"Hear, O Israel! The Lord is our God, the Lord is one!..."* The original Hebrew word used for "one" is *echad*, literally a "composite oneness," which is different from an absolute "one." The identical word, *echad*, appears in Genesis 2:24, where Adam and Eve are joined together to become "one flesh." Likewise, Ezekiel 37:14-19 uses *echad* to describe two sticks that become one in the prophet's hand. [17"]*Then join them for yourself one to another into one stick, that they may become one in your hand...."*

To a Christian, the meaning of the matzah becomes clear. The three pieces of matzah represent the Holy Trinity that is God: The Father, the Son, and the Holy Spirit. They are three, yet they are "one" as the word *echad* dictates. Christians do not serve multiple gods, only One, a point sometimes misunderstood by our Jewish brethren.

During the Passover Seder, the middle matzah that represents the Messiah who was prophesied to die is singled out, removed, and broken in two. The breaking of bread signifies death. Christ would be crucified just as the prophets had predicted in Psalm 22, Isaiah 53, and Daniel 9. In this way, Jesus gave new meaning to an old tradition, whose real purpose was hidden until the New Testament revelation.

Traditionally, half of the Afikomen is wrapped in white linen or placed in a bag called the *Matzo Tosh*, and hidden. At one point during the service, children search for this piece of unleavened bread. Whoever finds it brings it back to be redeemed for a price. The other half of the loaf is eaten, thus ending the meal. This demonstrates God's salvation, as Jesus taught when He proclaimed in John 6:51, *"I am the living bread that came down out of heaven; if anyone eats of this bread, he shall live forever; and the bread also which I shall give for the life of the world is My flesh."*

After the Seder, Christ and the disciples sang a hymn of praise. This hymn is known in Jewish tradition as the *Hallel*. It is taken from Psalm 118:22, which directly speaks of the Messiah: *The stone, which the builders rejected, has become the chief cornerstone.* Just one week earlier, Jesus had said that He was the stone that the builders rejected.[17]

Prophecy Fulfilled Following the Seder

The day of Passover began in the early evening immediately after the sun had set. The "day" would continue until the following evening at the same time. Shortly after the Passover meal, in the Garden of Gethsemane on the Mount of

---

[17] Matthew 21:42

Olives, Judas Iscariot returned to betray Jesus. Judas knew where the Messiah would be and that he would be alone. The authorities did not, which is why they needed Judas to locate and point him out to the temple guards who would take him away.

At 9 a.m. (the third hour) of the following morning, Jesus was crucified on the cross.[18] This sacrificial offering was made just as the first lamb of the daily offertory was laid upon the altar in the temple. The hour when the second lamb of the daily ceremony was brought out to the platform was 12 noon. It was at this moment that the sun went dark.[19] Then at the ninth hour (3 p.m.), the time for offering the second sacrifice, Jesus surrendered His life on the cross.[20]

In precise accordance with the Passover prophecy, Jesus became the fulfillment of that event. He did not fulfill just part of the prophecy; He fulfilled all of it. Christ was the Lamb of God who was given to set humanity free from the bondage of sin.[21] Buried on the Jewish Feast of Unleavened Bread, His voluntary offering on the cross protects us from eternal death.[22]

On the first day of the week, Christ rose from the dead, as prescribed by Mosaic Law for the day after the Sabbath of Passover week. It was the precise day when the Israelites celebrated the Feast of Firstfruits.[23] This feast designated the beginning of the harvest when the people presented the first fruits of their barley harvest to God.

---

[18] Mark 15:25
[19] Matthew 27:45; Mark 15:33; Luke 22:44
[20] Mark 15:33-34
[21] John 1:29; Psalm 22; Isaiah 53
[22] 1 Corinthians 5:7
[23] Leviticus 23:9-14

God specifically prescribed that this feast would always fall on a Sunday. Josephus, writing in *Antiquities of the Jews* around A.D. 80 or 90, stated that the Feast of First fruits had changed and that it always used to fall on the first day of the week, a Sunday.[24] At the time of Christ, it was a Sunday. Therefore, the day Christ rose from the dead was also symbolically the first day or period of Creation in Genesis (Saturday would have been the seventh day). On that first day, all of creation was renewed, beginning with Christ, who was raised from the dead to become the first fruits of those who were asleep.[25]

Summary

Jesus observed the Passover meal with His disciples before His crucifixion. His death was a fulfillment of the types and shadows in the Passover meal. Since the days of Adam and Eve, when God said

---

[24] Josephus, *Antiquities of the Jews*, 14.2.1, 17.9.3; Josephus, *The Wars of the Jews*, 5.3.1.
[25] 1 Corinthians 15:20

a "seed of Eve" would crush the head of the serpent (Satan), God had been pointing to an offering for sin that would be made by the Messiah. Jesus was that Messiah; the Passover substantiates that.

Just as God commanded the Hebrews to commemorate their deliverance from Egypt through observance of Passover, Christians were instructed by God (Christ) to remember His sacrifice continually through a celebration of the Lord's Supper (communion). Understanding the first leads to a much deeper understanding of the second.

CARRYING THE LAW FROM THE MOUNTAIN

CHAPTER 2
THE HISTORY OF PASSOVER

When the hour had come, He reclined at the table, and the apostles with Him. And He said to them, "I have earnestly desired to eat this Passover with you before I suffer.
Luke 22: 14–15

Passover is an annual occurrence, commanded by God, in commemoration of a significant event in the history of the Hebrew nation. The circumstances leading up to Passover are among the most dramatic of any in scripture in the Bible. Approximately 3,500 years ago, the Hebrew people found themselves as captives, enslaved in Egypt, a land where earlier under Joseph, they had been welcome. Their situation seemed hopeless, but it was in their darkest hour that God spoke to Moses from a burning bush that was not consumed by its fire. God declared that He was aware of the plight of His people and that He would rescue them from bondage and deliver them into the land promised to Abraham, Isaac, and Jacob.

Plague after plague was brought upon the Egyptians, but Pharaoh refused to let God's people go. Eventually, God struck at the very heart of Pharaoh's house, along with every other dwelling in Egypt. On an appointed night, the Lord's angel of death passed over the homes, taking the lives of the firstborn. However, those who had slain a lamb and applied its blood in a specified way over the door were spared. Hence, Israel was saved, but Pharaoh was not.

In frustration and desperation, Pharaoh relented and let the Israelites leave the land, taking their belongings with them, along with gifts solicited from willing Egyptians. It has been estimated that more than a million slaves, all carrying their possessions, marched from the land of Goshen, past the Sphinx of Egypt, and into the desert.[1] They would ultimately cross the Red Sea and wander the wilderness for forty years before reaching and entering the Promised Land. Yet, their salvation was not without cost. Blood had to be shed to secure this redemption.

The Hebrew deliverance and rescue from Egypt is symbolized in the Lord's first ordained feast and the sacrifice of the Passover lamb. Likewise, the world's redemption and escape from the second death required a "Passover Sacrifice," which was Jesus, the Lamb of God. The New Testament clearly alludes to Passover when Paul writes in 1 Corinthians 5:7, *Clean out the old leaven so that you may be a new lump, just as you are in fact unleavened. For Christ, our Passover also has been sacrificed.* This was plainly referenced in John 1:29: *The next day he saw Jesus coming to him and said, "Behold, the Lamb of God who takes away the sin of the world!"*

Passover is a remembrance of the time when the Lord's angel of death moved through Egypt killing the firstborn of all people and animals. This last plague that God visited upon Egypt compelled Pharaoh to release the Israelites from slavery and allow them to leave the country.

On the first night of Passover, God commanded the descendants of Abraham to take the blood of a blemish-free male lamb and brush it on the doorposts and lintels of their houses. When the Lord's angel saw the markings, he would "pass over" the house, sparing the occupants. Centuries later, the first Christians immediately saw this as a foreshadowing of the spotless Lamb of God whose blood would cover the sins of those who believed in Him. His sacrifice of blood on the cross would cause God's judgment to "pass over" them.

---

[1] Kevin Howard and Marvin Rosenthal, *The Feasts of the Lord* (Orlando, FL: Zion's Hope), pp. 17-18.

From the time of the first Passover until now, Jews have celebrated the event in remembrance of God's grace to them. Likewise, Christians take communion in celebration of the same forgiveness, because Christ was a sacrifice for the world; hence, he is called the Lamb of God.

The first Christians observed Passover, as did Jesus Christ. Luke 22 tells us that Jesus called his disciples to celebrate Passover, instructing Peter and John prepare the observance for the rest. Later in Luke, we read: [14]*When the hour had come, He reclined at the table, and the apostles with Him.*

Leonardo Da Vinci's Last Supper 1498 AD

My first exposure to a Passover Seder came as the result of a kind invitation from Nathan Kline, a close Jewish friend and business associate of mine. I'd been asking him questions about the Jewish celebration of Passover for months, so he arranged for me to attend one. At the event, I clearly saw what I believed to be a prominent Christian message. Nathan's kindness marked the beginning of my Passover journey. Many Passovers and hundreds of hours of research followed. As I understood more and more, I realized that the Passover celebration was an excellent educational tool. In fact, I was convinced that, without understanding Passover, one couldn't completely understand the nature of the Last Supper, Holy Communion, or the prophecies concerning Christ's death and resurrection.

The organization, *Jews for Jesus,* has long promoted Christian Passover services as a means for Messianic Jews to hold on to their cultural legacy while affirming their Christian faith. To their immense credit, they have also used the event to reach out to Christians, bringing together the Jewish and Christian beliefs by demonstrating the story of salvation through the ancient ceremony.

Hebrews 10 is an often-quoted scripture which clearly explains that the sacrificial killing of animals will not ultimately atone for sin. Advocates for and against celebrating a Christian Passover often quote parts of this scripture, but often leave out essential passages, which is why it is a good thing to read it in its entirety both for clarity and context:

Hebrews 10: 1-18

[1] *For the Law, since it has only a shadow of the good things to come and not the very form of things, can never, by the same sacrifices year by year, which they offer continually, make perfect those who draw near.* [2] *Otherwise, would they not have ceased to be offered, because the worshipers, having once been cleansed, would no longer have had consciousness of sins?* [3] *But in those sacrifices, there is a reminder of sins year by year.* [4] *For it is impossible for the blood of bulls and goats to take away sins.*

[5] *Therefore, when He comes into the world, He says, "Sacrifice and offering You have not desired, but a body You have prepared for Me;* [6] *in whole burnt offerings and sacrifices for sin You have taken no pleasure.* [7] *"Then I said, 'Behold, I have come (in the scroll of the book it is written of Me) to do Your will, O God.'"*

[8] *After saying above, "Sacrifices and offerings and whole burnt offerings and sacrifices for sin You have not desired, nor have You taken pleasure in them" (which are offered according to the Law),* [9] *then He said, "Behold, I have come*

to do Your will." He takes away the first in order to establish the second. [10] By this will we have been sanctified through the offering of the body of Jesus Christ once for all.
[11] Every priest stands daily ministering and offering time after time the same sacrifices, which can never take away sins; [12] but He, having offered one sacrifice for sins for all time, sat down at the right hand of God, [13] waiting from that time onward until His enemies be made a footstool for His feet. [14] For by one offering He has perfected for all time those who are sanctified.
[15] And the Holy Spirit also testifies to us; for after saying, [16] "This is the covenant that I will make with them after those days, says the Lord: I will put My laws upon their heart, and on their mind I will write them," He then says, [17] "And their sins and their lawless deeds I will remember no more." [18] Now where there is forgiveness of these things, there is no longer any offering for sin.

Clearly, the final atonement was that of Jesus Christ who alone offered the one sacrifice acceptable to God. In so doing, He became the intercessory high priest, replacing the prior sacrificial system. Understanding this moment in history provides a greater understanding of John 1:29: *The next day he saw Jesus coming to him and said, "Behold, the Lamb of God who takes away the sin of the world!"*

Who Provided the Sacrifice?

In the earlier Old Testament passages in Genesis 22, Abraham offers Isaac up as a sacrifice on the very mountain where Christ was crucified. One of the most exciting parts of the biblical passage appears in verses 7–8:

Genesis 22: 7–8
7 Isaac spoke to Abraham his father and said, "My father!" And he said, "Here I am, my son." And he said, "Behold, the fire, and the wood, but where is the lamb for the burnt offering?" 8 Abraham said, "God will provide for Himself the lamb for the burnt offering, my son." So the two of them walked on together.

The passage, *"God will provide for Himself the lamb for the burnt offering, my son."* is most striking. This was the New American Standard translation. An equally accurate King James translation reads:

[8] *And Abraham said, "My son, God will provide himself a lamb for a burnt offering."* By shifting our traditional point of view, but not changing the scripture, it seems to say that God will provide Himself as an offering, which is what He did. But, then, who else but God could have done this?

A similar event occurs in Revelation 5:2-5 (NIV): *[2]And I saw a mighty angel proclaiming in a loud voice, "Who is worthy to break the seals and open the scroll?" [3]But no one in heaven or on earth or under the earth could open the scroll or even look inside it. [4]I wept and wept because no one was found who was worthy to open the scroll or look inside. [5]Then one of the elders said to me, "Do not weep! See, the Lion of the tribe of Judah, the Root of David, has triumphed. He is able to open the scroll and its seven seals."* Once again, there was no one worthy, other than God who had made Himself the ultimate Passover sacrifice.[2]

The Passover Seder demonstrates how God keeps His promises and reveals Jesus as the coming Messiah. Scripture tells us that those things that happened to Israel are an example for us.[3] The Passover Seder speaks to both the Old and New Testaments.

---

[2] The Book of Mark describes how the temple priests were unable to convict Him, because their trumped-up charges became inconsistent and fell apart. Only when Jesus voluntarily answered, "I am!" to the question, "Are you the Son of God?" were they able to condemn Him. Even before Pilate, conviction became a political expedient. The Lamb of God went to the cross willingly as an innocent lamb led to slaughter. Thus, Jesus fulfilled the Passover and thousands of years of biblical prophecy.

[3] 1Corinthians 10: 11

**AN ANGEL PREVENTS ABRAHAM'S
SACRIFICE OF ISAAC.
Rembrandt, 1634**

Summary

Passover has been observed for over four thousand years. The event was given special meaning by Jesus' instructions to keep the Lord's Supper in memory of His sacrificial death on the cross. Although many centuries have passed, the Jewish Passover of ancient times continues to point to Yeshua *(Jesus)* as the Messiah and as our Salvation.

AND HE WENT A LITTLE BEYOND THEM, AND FELL ON HIS FACE AND PRAYED, SAYING, "MY FATHER, IF IT IS POSSIBLE, LET THIS CUP PASS FROM ME; YET NOT AS I WILL, BUT AS YOU WILL." *Matthew 26:39*

A Passover tells us what Jesus' Last Supper was like, and it is through the Passover that the Christian learns the historical significance of the communion elements.

Matthew 26:26–28

[26] *While they were eating, Jesus took some bread, and after a blessing, He broke it and gave it to the disciples, and said, "Take, eat; this is My body."* [27] *And when He had taken a cup and given thanks, He gave it to them, saying, "Drink from it, all of you;* [28] *for this is My blood of the covenant, which is poured out for many for forgiveness of sins."*

CHAPTER 3
SHOULD CHRISTIANS KEEP PASSOVER?

"Speak to the sons of Israel and say to them, 'The LORD'S appointed times which you shall proclaim as holy convocations - My appointed times are these: 'For six days' work may be done, but on the seventh day there is a Sabbath of complete rest, a holy convocation. You shall not do any work; it is a Sabbath to the LORD in all your dwellings. 'These are the appointed times of the LORD, holy convocations which you shall proclaim at the times appointed for them."
Leviticus 23:2–4

People worldwide celebrate holidays. Even the most primitive of peoples has its special days for celebration. Throughout all creation, there are thousands of annual holidays. By contrast, God has only seven. It's not wrong for us to have other holidays, yet many people are not aware of the seven as set aside in scripture. These seven holidays, called "the feasts of the Lord" are discussed throughout the Bible in both the Old and New Testaments. All seven are listed in chronological sequence in the 23rd chapter of Leviticus. The expression "Feasts of the Lord" clearly indicates that these are God's holidays, but that He has made them available to us. On His terms, we may enter into their benefit.

The timing of the seven feasts is based upon the Jewish lunar calendar of 354-day years. Every 19 years, their annual chronicle had the 13th month to make up for the shorter years. Consequently, the holidays do not fall on the same day as on the Gregorian calendar (the one we use today).

The seven feasts of the Lord are prophetic, a fact recognized by Bible scholars since the time of Christ. To the Christian, the holidays begin with Passover, at the cross where Jesus willingly gave himself as a sacrifice for the world's sins.

"These are the appointed Feasts of the LORD, the holy convocations." Leviticus 23:4

1. **Feast of Passover**
   (Pesach) - 14th of Nisan

2. **Feast of Unleavened Bread**
   (Hag haMatzot) - 21st of Nisan

3. **Feast of Firstfruits - *the grain harvest***
   (Yom haBikkurim) - 16th of Nisan

4. **Feast of Weeks,**
   Pentecost (Shavuot) - 6th of Sivan

5. **Feast of Trumpets**
   (Yom Teruah, Rosh ha-Shanah) - 1st or 2nd of Tishri

6. **Day of Atonement**
   (Yom Kippur) - 10th of Tishri

7. **Feast of Tabernacles**
   (Sukkot) - 15th to 21st of Tishri

* Many Christian Scholars believe that Jesus fulfilled the prophecy of the first four feasts at His first coming. Messianic Jews and a growing number of Christians expect that he will fulfill the remaining three at His second coming *(to be discussed in this and succeeding chapters)*

THE APPOINTED FEASTS OF THE LORD

They reach a climax during the Feast of Tabernacles, which symbolizes the Kingdom of the Messiah's second coming.

Nothing in the feasts requires a Christian to twist words or manipulate the truth. All people have been invited to meet with God and receive the blessings toward which His Feasts point. This is a blessing. This should not surprise us as Gentiles. It is consistent with God's declaration in Genesis 22:18 that through Abraham all nations would be blessed: *"In your seed, all the nations of the earth shall be blessed because you have obeyed My voice."* Likewise, Christ taught us in John 4:22 that *"Salvation is from the Jews."*

About the Sevens

Seven is historically the biblical number for perfection. The world was created in seven periods or days (the Hebrew word *yom* is used, meaning either a day or an undefined period). The seventh day was a day of rest for God and for humanity. The Jewish Jubilee year was defined as seven sevens of years (or 49) with the 50th year the Jubilee year. After the Jubilee year, all debts were forgiven, and slaves set free. Revelation uses the number seven some 350 times, as it discusses the seven seals, trumpets, and bowls.

The seven feasts are also referred to as the "appointed times" during which God will meet with humans for divine purposes. Many biblical scholars believe that when the "appointed times prophecies" are completed, they bring this age to an end and usher in the golden age, which is to follow.

Why Christians Should Consider Celebrating Passover

Four of the seven holidays occur during the spring of the year, and the remaining three, in the fall. The initial four depict events associated with Christ's first coming, while the final ones are related to specific circumstances in His second coming.

The beginning of the seven feasts is Passover. It is the foundational spiritual holiday, and the others that follow are built upon it. The objective of this book is to explore and explain that feast day, as well as to describe how the Christian may celebrate it in a church setting or in the home.

Today, most Christians do not celebrate Passover, since many see it as belonging to the Old Testament or to Jewish traditions that they believe are no longer necessary. Among the Christians who do, there are divergent schools of thought as to why, and we will explore several reasons.

God chose to reveal Himself through Israel, His creation and His Son Jesus. God promised that He would bless all nations through Abraham, and from the land of Israel would arrive, the Messiah. The message was explicit, not just in Genesis 12:1-3 but also in John 4:22: *"...We worship what we know, for salvation is from the Jews."*

Passover was and is a shadow of what was and is to come. For the observant Christian, it is an ancient prophecy fulfilled. Jew and Christian realize that through prophecy, God foretells the future so that others witnessing its fulfillment may believe. God proclaimed, *"...There is no one like Me...Declaring the end from the beginning, And, from ancient times the things which have not been done."* [1]

We must bear in mind that Jesus was Jewish, as were most of the early Christians. Obviously one can be Jewish and a Christian.

---

[1] Isaiah 46: 9,10

Whether a Christian celebrates the day, Passover is a matter of conscience for the individual Christian. All of God's appointed feasts are a foreshadowing of Christ's life, death, and resurrection. The apostle Paul was unmistakable when he wrote in Colossians 2:16-17, [16] *Therefore no one is to act as your judge regarding food or drink or in respect to a festival or a new moon or a Sabbath day-* [17] *things which are a mere shadow of what is to come; but the substance belongs to Christ.*

It is very beneficial for a Christian to celebrate Passover because it leads to a greater understanding and appreciation of Christ's atonement for us, as well as our deliverance from the servitude of sin. While Christians are not bound to observe Passover, the way Jews of the Old Testament did, or as Orthodox Jews do today, non-observing Christians should, nonetheless, not belittle those who do. It is painful to hear Christians use phrases like, "We don't want to be Judaized," or, "Don't Judaize this church." Fortunately, I have not heard this often but enough to mention it. Christians who say such things obviously forget that Christ was a Jew. It is useful to remind such people of the words of Jesus from John 4:22: *"You worship what you do not know; we worship what we know, for salvation is from the Jews."* Therefore, lest we become disparaging to the point of missing Christ's words, we should evaluate our feelings carefully and honestly.

Romans 14:3-6
[3] *The one who eats is not to regard with contempt the one who does not eat, and the one who does not eat is not to judge the one who eats, for God has accepted him.* [4] *Who are you to judge the servant of another? To his own master he stands or falls; and he will stand, for the Lord is able to make him stand.* [5] *One person regards one day above another, another regards every day alike. Each person must be fully convinced in his own mind.* [6] *He who observes the*

day, observes it for the Lord, and he who eats, does so for the Lord, for he gives thanks to God; and he who eats not, for the Lord he does not eat, and gives thanks to God.

A Tale of Two Faiths

Christians aren't the only ones resenting other Christians' observation of Passover. There is pushback from some in the Jewish community. Such resistance must be met with love and sound reasoning. How should one answer criticism that may come from our Jewish brethren? I begin with Leviticus 23:2: *"Speak to the sons of Israel and say to them, 'The LORD'S appointed times which you shall proclaim as holy convocations -My appointed times are these."*

I always emphasize the critical use of the word "my" in the previous scripture verse. It clearly states that the "feasts" are the Lord's, not that of man. Biblically, they don't belong to any specific denomination or racial designation. The Christian may partake of the Passover, as can one of the Jewish-faith.

Many years ago, following a Passover I had conducted, several Jewish men in attendance approached me with a question. They asked where I found the name Jesus in the Hebrew Bible. It was a good question, the answer to which may be helpful to other Christians.

Dr. Elias E. Hidalgo, with the *Shalom Scripture Studies, Inc.,* wrote that the question of Jesus' name in the Hebrew text is one that often occurs when Jews and Christians gather to talk. Because we are looking at Christ in the Passover as a part of Passover history, it is appropriate that we take time to discuss it.[2]

The Name of Jesus (ישוע) in The Old Testament

Jesus
Yeh-SHU-ah
יֵשׁוּעַ

---

[2] Elias E. Hidalgo, *Y'SHUA in the Tanach* (Savannah, GA: Shalom Scripture Studies, 1995).

In his discussion of Christ's name in the Hebrew biblical text, Dr. Elias E. Hidalgo provided an excellent summary of verses. He pointed out that Jesus is spoken of in the Hebrew Bible in Isaiah 7:14, Isaiah 9:6, Micah 5:2 and elsewhere. He wrote that it was common in Hebrew to give a child a name with meaning.[3]   In Genesis 5:29, Lamech called his son Comfort *(Noah)*, saying, "...*This one will give us rest from our work and from the toil of our hands arising from the ground which the Lord has cursed.*" Again, in Exodus 2:10, Pharaoh's daughter called the baby rescued from the Nile "Drawn-Forth" or Moses. She said, "...Because I drew him out of the water."

We find similar examples in Genesis 25:24-26, "*And when her days to be delivered were fulfilled, behold, there were twins in her womb. Now the first came out red, all over like a hairy garment; and they named him Esau. Afterward, his brother forth with his hand holding on to Esau's heel, so his name was called Jacob...*" So, one can appreciate the fact that the man Jacob at his birth was called *Heel* because he grabbed hold of his brother's heel! Throughout the Bible, there are many examples of such naming of children. But what about the name of Jesus in the Hebrew Bible? Is it there?

The Hebrew name, Y'shua (which in Greek was translated as Jesus) is frequently found in the Jewish text of the Tanach (the Old Testament). The name Y'shua means "salvation"!

Examples

Before the birth of Christ, the Lord's angel spoke to Joseph, soon to be the husband of Mary, the mother of Jesus. The angel said, "*But when he had considered this, behold, an angel of the Lord appeared to him in a dream, saying, "Joseph,*

---

[3] Ibid.

son of David, do not be afraid to take Mary as your wife; for the Child who has been conceived in her is of the Holy Spirit. [21] *"She will bear a Son; and you shall call His name Jesus, for He will save His people from their sins."* [22] *Now all this took place to fulfill what was spoken by the Lord through the prophet..."* In other words, the angel was saying that Mary would bring forth a child (Y'shua) and that He would be called "salvation", for that was his purpose.

Within the New Testament can be found the Old Testament revealed. In reverse, within the Old Testament can be found the New Testament concealed, as we shall see in the following verses:[4]

1. In Genesis 49, Jacob nears his death and calls his children together to prophesy over them. At the end of Dan's prophecy (verse 18), Jacob says, *"[18] For Your salvation I wait, O LORD...."* What he said was, "For Your Y'shua (Jesus), I am waiting (or looking)."

2. In David's psalm of thanksgiving (Psalm 9), the king of Israel says, [13] *Be gracious to me, O LORD; See my affliction from those who hate me, You who lift me up from the gates of death,* [14] *That I may tell of all Your praises, That in the gates of the daughter of Zion I may rejoice in Your salvation.* Translated, David said, "I will rejoice in Your Y'shua (Jesus)."

3. Y'shua (Jesus) is written three times in Isaiah 12: 2-3, [2] *"Behold, God is my salvation, I will trust and not be afraid; For the LORD GOD is my strength and song, And He has become my salvation.* [3] *Therefore you will joyously draw water from the springs of salvation.* "To put it another way, Isaiah is writing that, "God is my Y'shua *(Jesus)*. I will keep the faith and be unafraid because the Lord is also my

---

[4] Missler, Chuck, How to Study the Bible, Koinonia House, 1992, pp. 19-42

Y'shua (Jesus). So, it is with joy that water shall be drawn from the wells of Y'shua (Jesus)."

In this verse, we see that Y'shua is God, and he is to become our Y'shua (Jesus) so that the wells of salvation (Y'shua) are the waters of salvation.

4. Remarkably, Isaiah 62:11 reads, "[11] *Behold, the LORD has proclaimed to the end of the earth, say to the daughter of Zion, 'Lo, your salvation comes; Behold His reward is with Him, and His recompense before Him.'"* In this verse, we see that the Lord proclaims to the ends of the earth and the Jewish people, "Look, your salvation (Y'shua or Jesus) comes and He brings His reward with him as His work is before Him."

Clearly, the Hebrew word Y'shua is a person, not a thing or an event. Dr. Hidalgo very ably points out in Habakkuk 3:13 an even greater demonstration of the name of Jesus in the Tanach, "[13] *You went forth for the salvation of Your people, For the salvation of Your anointed. You struck the head of the house of the evil to lay him open from thigh to neck. Selah.*"

The word for anointed is *Messiah*, which is the same as the English "Christ" or "Anointed One." So, in looking at the previous verse, we can see that the name of Y'shua HaMassiach (Jesus the Christ) is in the Tanach (Old Testament). Moreover, Jesus is doing what Genesis 3:15 had predicted that 'the Seed of the Woman' would do, as stated in Habakkuk 3:13, wounding the head of the wicked.

We have mentioned only a few of about 75 references in the Old Testament that speak of Y'shua or Jesus as a Person. Could this be a coincidence?

Perhaps in a future Bible study, you might wish to search out the others. It is instructive, as I have personally discovered, and a valuable witnessing tool.

The question remains, however: should Christians keep Passover?

If we briefly consider the two faiths, Christianity and Judaism, we find them intertwined. The primary difference separating the two is that most Jews believe the Messiah is yet to come. Christians understand that He has already come and will come a second time. To the Christian that Messiah is Jesus Christ, but to the Jewish faith, He remains unknown. Bear in mind that the earliest Christians were Jews, just like the Man from Galilee.

Early in Christian church history, Christ's disciples preached and brought their testimony into the Jewish temple and synagogues. Thousands heard their message and became Christians. As time passed, though, the distance between the Jewish influence and Christianity grew wider, especially after the Roman destruction of the Temple in A.D. 70

A BRIEF CHURCH HISTORY

Constantine and the Council of Nicaea

There was little attempt to centralize the Church during its early years of formation. Contrary to popular opinion, even the Roman Emperor, Flavius Valerius Aurelius Constantinus (Constantine), who converted to Christianity in A.D. 312, didn't force the issue.[5] After his conversion, Constantine did issue edicts of toleration for Christianity, which ended centuries of murderous persecution.[6]

Constantine assembled the Council of Nicaea in Bithynia (present-day İznik, Turkey), in A.D. 325. This was a collection of prominent Christian bishops, who sought to gain consensus in the churches through an assembly

---

[5] Henry Wace and William C. Piercy, eds., "Constantine the Great," *Dictionary of Christian Biography and Literature to the Sixth Century*, (London: John Murray, 1911).
[6] Eamon Duffy, *Saints and Sinners* (1997), pp. 214–216.

representing all of Christendom.[7] The various Christian churches were engaged in escalating theological quarrels and controversy, resulting in increasing disunity among the Church leadership.

The Roman Empire was failing by A.D. 300, and Constantine realized that the empire could no longer withstand a division created by years of rampant doctrinal differences. He viewed the problem as a threat to Christianity and to Roman society but placed his emphasis on consensus, and so he did not attempt to force Roman views on the assembly. He demanded, however, that Christians settle their internal differences and become Christ-like agents who could convey new life into a troubled, demoralized realm.

CONSTANTINE, Bronze, Roman
Artwork, 4th Century BC

The main theological issue and focus at the Council of Nicaea were on Christ. Since the end of the Apostolic Age and the beginning of the Church Age, church leaders questioned, debated and quarreled over the question, "Who is the Christ?" They puzzled whether He was more divine than human or vice versa. As the Son of God, was Jesus co-equal with God, or less than God and lower in status? Was the Lord God the One and only true God; or

---

[7] Richard Kieckhefer, "Papacy," *Dictionary of the Middle Ages* (American Council of Learned Societies, 1989).

were the Father, the Son, and the Holy Spirit, combined, the One true God?

After the Council began, Constantine demanded that the bishops make a majority decision defining precisely who Jesus Christ was. Constantine required that they create a "creed doctrine" that Christianity would follow a doctrine called the "Nicene Creed," to be upheld by the Church and enforced by the emperor. The bishops decreed the full deity of Christ as the accepted position for the Church. The Council of Nicaea voted to make the Trinity the official doctrine of the Church. Note that the Council of Nicaea did not invent these doctrines. Instead, it recognized what the Bible taught, and afterward, the Council systematized the doctrines.

Some of the doctrines decided upon by the Council of Nicaea included the following:

- The New Testament teaches that Jesus the Messiah should be worshiped and trusted, acknowledging He is co-equally God and man.
- The New Testament forbids the worship of angels[8] but commands a reverence of Christ.
- The Apostle Paul tells us that in Christ "all the fullness of the Deity lives in bodily form."[9]
- Paul declares Jesus as Lord and the One to whom a person must pray for salvation just as one calls on Jehovah, Yahweh.[10]
- Jesus is God, "over all"[11] and our God and Savior.[12] Faith in Jesus' deity was basic to Paul's

---

[8] Colossians 2:18; Revelation 22:8, 9
[9] Colossians 2:9, 1:19
[10] Joel 2:32; Romans 10:9-13
[11] Romans 9:5

testimony and theology and therefore became part of the Nicaea Doctrine.

The Council supported John's gospel, which declares Jesus to be:

- The Divine eternal agent of creation and source of life and light;[13] as stated in, "the way, the truth, and the life";[14]

- An advocate with the Heavenly Father;[15] as sovereign;[16] the rider on a white horse;[17] and the totality of the Son of God from the beginning to the end.[18]

The Council of Nicaea did not invent the doctrine of the Deity of Christ. Instead, they affirmed the apostles' teaching of who Christ was and is—the One true God, with the Father and the Holy Spirit. The council settled the differences between the various churches of the time; however, the distance between Jews and the Church had already widened and would continue to do so.

By the Middle Ages, antipathy toward the Jews grew at an unprecedented rate, fueled in part by an uneducated population relying on information supplied them through an ever-increasingly centralized Church. The Church overlooked that Roman leadership ultimately ordered Jesus' crucifixion. To be sure, the temple leaders of the time were involved, but

---

[12] Titus 2:13
[13] John 1:1-5, 9
[14] John 14:6
[15] 1 John 2:1-2
[16] Revelation 1:5
[17] Revelation 19:11-16
[18] Revelation 22:13

even they were political appointments made by and through a Roman-appointed King Herod.

Racial bias against the Jews spread, carrying over into Martin Luther's Protestant reformation movement in the 16th century.[19] Consequently, many Christians of that era abandoned all of Judaism without good reason. Scores of Christians denounced all Jewish teaching based on the reasoning that "We are not bound by the law." Yet so many remained unaware of what the law was.

Today, we may look back with a far more precise and less biased view of history than our ancestors could. It is also possible to explore much of the past that has become part of our current religious thought.

Christians and the Jewish Conflict

In A.D. 70, the Romans destroyed Jerusalem and the temple along with it. Before the onslaught, those Christians—sensing elements of Christ's prophecy regarding certain end-time events—fled the city, with many to Petra. By so doing, they avoided the Roman slaughter in Jerusalem as well as the dispersion. Jews unfamiliar with the prophecy, however, saw the fleeing Christians as deserters. This combined with earlier Christian persecution, the die was cast, and the prejudice between the faiths grew, continuing in some churches today.

Many Christians today read their New Testament scriptures on a regular basis but frequently ignore the Old Testament. Years ago, I had a long, in-depth discussion with a devoutly Christian man who confessed; "I don't read the Old

---

[19] Martin Luther, *Man Between God and the Devil*, trans. Heiko A. Oberman (New Haven: Yale University, 1989), pp. 54-158.

Testament, because the apostle Paul declared that we are no longer under the Law because Christ's death and resurrection made the Law passé." Is that what Paul was saying? The answer is "no," as we shall soon see.

Paul's reference to the Law encompassed far more than God's Ten Commandments or the Torah (the original five books of the Bible). Christians in the first century knew of and understood the expansive nature of Jewish Law.

By New Testament times, Jewish spiritual leaders had enlarged the scope of the Law by quite some measure. Many writings of previous rabbis had become elevated to the level of the Law so that these "laws" during Christ's era were burdensome, to put it mildly. Keep in mind that these writings were different from the Law brought down from Mount Sinai.

It is important to note that not all the Jewish faith agree on these issues. On the contrary, just as the Christian faith had its divisions so did Judaism. The Pharisees, the Sadducees and the Essenes all saw the Law differently. The Sadducees, during the Second Temple period, rejected the belief in the resurrection of the dead, a central tenet believed by Pharisees and early Christians, which provoked increasing hostilities.[20]

Furthermore, the Sadducees rejected the Oral Law as proposed by the Pharisees. Instead, the Sadducees saw the Torah as the sole source of divine authority.[21] The expanded, written law, in its depiction of the priesthood, corroborated the power and enforced the supremacy of the Sadducees in Judean society. For them, the more rules, the better. This seems to be a similar theme put forward by many in the modern era as well.

> **The more things change, the more they stay the same!**
> **Jean-Baptiste Alphonse Karr, 1849**

---

[20] Mark 12:18
[21] Flavius Josephus, *Josephus: Translation and Commentary*, p. 130.

The main antagonists of the Sadducees were the Pharisees,[22] a more conservative group of which Paul was a member. Josephus (A.D. 37–c. 100), also a Pharisee, claimed that Pharisees received the backing and goodwill of the ordinary people, apparently in contrast to the more elite Sadducees.[23] In turn, Pharisees claimed prophetic or Mosaic authority for their interpretation of Jewish laws. The Essenes, on the other hand, were even more scripturally based and challenged the authenticity of the rule of the Sadducees, blaming the downfall of ancient Israel and the siege of Jerusalem on their impiety. The Essenes gained fame in modern times because of the discovery of the Dead Sea Scrolls, which they had hidden in a cave near the Dead Sea.[24] [25]

Today, as before, modern Judaism and Christianity have both maintained denominational differences and practices. Just as Christian Communion is practiced differently among the various church denominations, Passover is also celebrated in multiple ways within Jewish households of varying synagogues.[26]

Christianity and Judaism Today

Historically, Judaism claims a continuity spanning more than 3,000 years and is considered the oldest monotheistic religion still in existence.[27] Many aspects of Judaism have directly or indirectly influenced the world's secular Western ethics and civil laws.[28]

---

[22] Cecil Roth, *A History of the Jews: From Earliest Times Through the Six Day War* (1970), p. 180.

[23] Flavius Josephus, *Antiquity of the Jews*.

[24] F.F. Bruce, *Second Thoughts on the Dead Sea Scrolls* (Paternoster Press, 1956).

[25] Lawrence H. Schiffman, "Essenes," *Reclaiming the Dead Sea Scrolls* (Philadelphia: Jewish Publication Society, 1994).

[26] Diarmaid MacCulloch, *The Reformation: A History* (New York: Penguin Books, 2004), pp. 84-117.

[27] "Religion & Ethics—Judaism," BBC, 2010-08-22.

[28] Joseph Jacobs, *Jewish Contributions to Civilization: An Estimate* (Philadelphia: Jewish Publication Society of America, 1920), pp. 12-24.

The major Jewish movements are Orthodox Judaism (consisting of Haredi Judaism and Modern Orthodox Judaism), Conservative Judaism and Reform Judaism. Their differences lie in their approach to Jewish Law. Orthodox Judaism maintains that the Torah and Jewish Law, divine in origin, eternal, and unalterable, must be strictly followed. The more liberal Conservative and Reform Judaism promote a more "traditional" interpretation of Judaism's requirements. One common position is that Jewish Law should be viewed as a set of guidelines, rather than as a set of restrictions and obligations that all Jews must observe.[29]

Traditionally, special courts enforced Jewish Law. To some extent, they still exist today, but the practice of Judaism is mostly voluntary.[30] No longer is an authority on theological or legal matters vested in any one individual or entity, but in the sacred texts and the rabbis and scholars who interpret them.[31]

Christianity expanded throughout the world during the Age of Exploration, a period starting in the early 15th century and continuing into the

---

[29] *Reform Judaism*, Religion/Facts,
http://www.religionfacts.com/judaism/denominations/reform.htm
[30] *Encyclopedia Britannica*. "Britannica Online Encyclopedia: Bet Din," Britannica.com 2011-08-22.
[31] "Judaism 101: Rabbis, Priests and Other Religious Functionaries," Jewfaq.org 2011-02-07

17th century when Europeans searched into Africa, the Americas, Asia, and Oceania. [32]

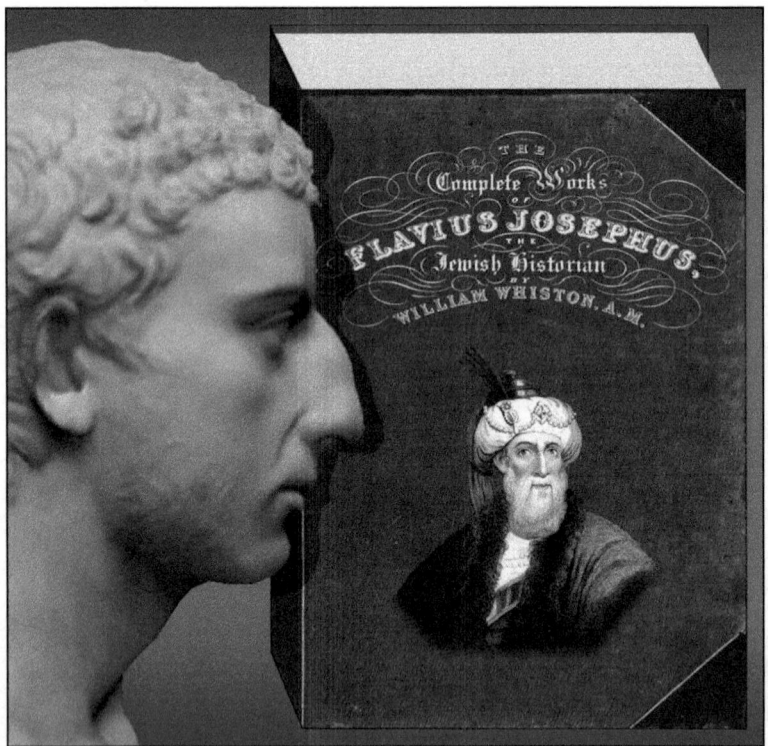

TITUS FLAVIUS JOSEPHUS (37–c. 100) was a 1st-century Romano-Jewish historian and man of letters, born in Jerusalem[33]—then part of Roman Judea—to a father of priestly descent and a mother who claimed royal ancestry.[34] A witness of the sack of Jerusalem, his most important works was *The Jewish War* and *Antiquities of the Jews*[35]. The *Jewish War* recounts the

---

[32] David Arnold, *The Age of Discovery, 1400–1600*, Lancaster pamphlets. (Routledge, 2002).
[33] Louis Feldman & Steve Mason, *Flavius Josephus* (Brill Academic Publishers, 1999).
[34] Stephen L. Harris, *Understanding the Bible* (Palo Alto: Mayfield, 1985).
[35] Ibid.

Jewish revolt against Roman occupation (A.D. 66–70), while Antiquities of the Jews tells the history of the world from a Jewish perspective for an ostensibly Roman audience.[36]

Christianity has since become the world's largest religion.[37] It differs most significantly from other faiths in its claim that Jesus Christ is God the Son; but throughout its history, Christianity has weathered schisms and theological disputes that resulted in many different believing churches. The largest branches of Christianity are the Roman Catholic Church, the Eastern Orthodox Church, and the Protestant Church.

After centuries of feuding, Judaism and evangelical Christianity, have become more united through many of their shared beliefs rather than their differences. Israel remains America's principal ally in the Middle East, as well as a primary trading partner.[38]

The overriding spiritual theme of Passover is one of salvation. This gives Passover an eternal meaning and holy significance. The sacrificial element is brought to its ultimate New Testament fulfillment in the sacrificial death of Christ, as God's promised sacrificial Lamb. During the first Passover, each Israelite was prepared for redemption, and in that exists a lesson for us all. Chapter 9 explores Passover's significance and symbolism in more detail, but we should first understand the events of the holy day to appreciate their relevance better. Chapters 2-8 first examine the circumstances and mechanisms for conducting Passover.

---

[36] Robert Karl Gnuse, *Dreams & Dream Reports in the Writings of Josephus: A Traditio-Historical Analysis* (E. J. Brill, 1996), pp. 136-142.
[37] "Religions by Adherents," Adherents.com
[38] "Israeli-United States Relations," adapted from a report by Clyde R. Mark, Congressional Research Service (17 October 2002).

The Christian Meaning of Passover

Summary

Passover is the foundational holiday for God's seven Feasts or "Appointed Times." Four of the Appointed Times occur in the spring and three in the winter.

There has been an outbreak of interest among Christians seeking to demonstrate a significant relationship between the observation of Passover and the death, burial, and resurrection of Jesus. A Christian celebration of the Passover provides a unique way to bring the story of salvation to prophetic life.

Whether a Christian celebrates Passover, is a matter of choice for the individual Christian. As with all the Old Testament Jewish feasts, the Passover Feast was a foreshadowing of Christ's atoning work on the cross. Although Christians are not required to celebrate Passover, studying about it leads to a greater understanding and appreciation for Christ's death and resurrection. The Passover presents a remarkable portrait of Christ's atonement and our deliverance from the bondage of sin.

As believing Christians, we should celebrate this gift—every day of our lives.

Exodus 12: 7

"Moreover, they shall take some of the blood and put it on the two doorposts and on the lintel of the houses in which they eat it."

CHAPTER 4
PASSOVER AND THE CHRISTIAN FAITH

Jews have celebrated Passover for more than four thousand years. The message it carries is as powerful today as it was when it first began. It provides Christians with the background to understand the Passover in the Upper Room, now called "the Last Supper." It gives additional meaning to Jesus' death on the cross and resurrection from the tomb.

Under the Law of Moses, Jews were required to celebrate the Passover every year to remember the Exodus from Egypt. When Jesus broke the bread, and drank the cup with His disciples, it was part of the Passover meal. Scripture is clear on this point. The meal should be important to Christians, because many ceremonial elements in the Passover point directly to the sacrifice that would be made by an expected Messiah who would rescue the world from slavery and sin.

Passover Symbolism to the Jewish Nation:

God used the Passover memorial as a time of praise for Israel's redemption from Egyptian slavery and a time of expectation for the era to come. By studying the journey that the Hebrews made, from their escape from Egypt to their entry into the Promised Land, we witness another journey, a journey through the wilderness of life to entry into the promised Kingdom of God.

Life as a Journey Through a Wilderness

1. God gave His people freedom from bondage.
2. He gave them victory over their enemies.
3. He fed them that they might live.
4. He did not leave them to wander the wilderness alone.
5. He led them by His presence in the day and His glory at night.
6. He gave them rules to bring order to their lives.
7. He provided for their healing.
8. He gave them forgiveness.
9. He gave them a weekly day of rest.
10. At the end of their journey, He brought them into the Promised Land—a land flowing with milk and honey.

From the time of Moses, Jews have celebrated the Passover in the same way, with only a few exceptions. The celebration itself is called a *Seder*. In Hebrew, the word means, "order." There is a set order of service that has scarcely varied for more than forty centuries.

The Historical Passover Order of Service

While there are variations in the sequence of the Seder, most services tend to observe the following order:

1. An initial blessing is said over the first of four cups of wine to be used during the meal.

2. Next, water is poured over the hands in a ceremonial purification.

3. A vegetable dipped in salt water, representing tears of the enslaved Hebrew, is eaten.

4. The second matzah of three (the unleavened bread) is broken in two. One of the broken halves is hidden until after the meal.

5. The story of the Passover is told, and a second cup of wine is poured and later drunk.

6. A second ritual washing of the hands may occur.

7. A blessing for the matzah is given.

8. The matzah is eaten.

9. Bitter herbs are eaten. In Hebrew, the bitter herbs are called *maror*. They are usually grated horseradish or lettuce. The scripture in Exodus 12:8 instructs the Jews to eat the lamb with unleavened bread and with bitter herbs.

10. A special "Hallel sandwich" is prepared and eaten.

11. The festival meal is eaten.

12. The broken matzah (the *Afikomen*) that was hidden is "discovered" and eaten.

13. A third cup of wine is poured and later drunk.

14. Psalms of praise are sung. Normally, they are taken from Psalm 113 to 118 (the *Hallel*). The pouring of a fourth cup of wine, which remains but is not consumed, follows.

15. After the meal, a final blessing is given, and all pray for peace in Jerusalem.

The Cups of Passover

The four cups of wine at Passover represent the four promises that God made to Israel. The first cup, the Cup of Sanctification, commemorates God's promise: "I will bring you out." The second cup, the Cup of Iniquities or Plagues, pertains to the plagues that fell upon Egypt at the time of the Exodus. Moreover, it represents God's second promise: "I will free you from being slaves." The third cup, the Cup of Redemption, remembers God's promise: "I will redeem you." It is here that Jesus announced the new covenant for the forgiveness of sins.[1]

---

[1] Similar explanations given in early 19th & 20th Century Haggadahs.

The 4 Cups of Passover

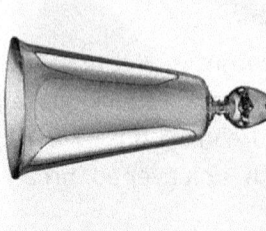

The First Cup
Cup of Sanctification

When the hour came, Jesus and his apostles reclined at the table. And he said to them, "I have eagerly desired to eat this Passover with you before I suffer.
Luke 22: 14,15

As the Lord set aside and sanctified the Israelites, so Christ set aside and sanctified those called by his name.

The Second Cup
Cup of Iniquity

Carrying his own cross, he went out to the place of the Skull (which in Aramaic is called Golgotha). 18 There they crucified him, and with him two others—one on each side and Jesus in the middle.
John 17,18

Just as God rescued Israel from Egypt's wrath, so He delivered us from sin's iniquity and wrath.

The Third Cup
Cup of Redemption

"In the same way, after the supper, Jesus took the cup, saying, "This cup is the new covenant in my blood, which is poured out for you. As often as you drink of it, do so in remembrance of Me."
Luke 22:20

It is with this Third Cup, with which the Lord Jesus initiated the practice of Communion in rememberence of Him.

The Fourth Cup
Cup of Taking Out

"For I tell you I will not drink again of the fruit of the vine until the kingdom of God comes.'
Luke 22:18

To be drank as promised at the second coming of the Messiah before the arrival of God's Millennium.

Matthew 26:26-28

[26] *While they were eating, Jesus took some bread, and after a blessing, He broke it and gave it to the disciples, and said, "Take, eat; this is My body."* [27] *And when He had taken a cup and given thanks, He gave it to them, saying, "Drink from it, all of you;* [28] *for this is My blood of the covenant, which is poured out for many for forgiveness of sins.*

The final, fourth cup, the Cup of Redemption or Completion, recalls God's promise that "I will take you as my own people." Jesus did not drink the fourth cup of wine. Instead, He said that He would drink that cup in heaven with those who followed Him.

Matthew 26:29

"But I say to you, I will not drink of this fruit of the vine from now on until that day when I drink it new with you in My Father's kingdom."

Other significant events in the service carry huge importance for the Christian faith. For example, at the place in the meal where bitter herbs are eaten, Jesus revealed that Judas would betray him:

There is much to be learned from each of the four cups and the ceremonies surrounding them.

Following the Cup of Completion, the Jews sang the Hallel or praise psalms that would end with Psalm 118. Indeed, Christ and the disciples did just that:

Matthew 26:30

After singing a hymn, they went out to the Mount of Olives.

The use of Psalm 118 is significant, because it happens to be one of the great Messianic passages in the Old Testament:

Psalm 118:14-26
[14] *The LORD is my strength and song, And He has become my salvation.*
[15] *The sound of joyful shouting and salvation is in the tents of the righteous; The right hand of the LORD does valiantly.* [16] *The right hand of the LORD is exalted; The right hand of the LORD does valiantly.* [17] *I will not die, but live, And tell of the works of the LORD.* [18] *The LORD has disciplined me severely, But He has not given me over to death.*
[19] *Open to me the gates of righteousness; I shall enter through them, I shall give thanks to the LORD.* [20] *This is the gate of the LORD; The righteous will enter through it.* [21] *I shall give thanks to You, for You have answered me, And You have become my salvation.*
[22] *The stone which the builders rejected Has become the chief corner stone.* [23] *This is the LORD'S doing; It is marvelous in our eyes.* [24] *This is the day which the LORD has made; Let us rejoice and be glad in it.* [25] *O LORD, do save, we beseech You; O LORD, we beseech You, do send prosperity!* [26] *Blessed is he who comes in the name of the LORD.*

Christians will recall that when Jesus made His triumphal entry into Jerusalem on Palm Sunday, the crowds acclaimed Him.

Matthew 21:6-11
[6] *The disciples went and did just as Jesus had instructed them,* [7] *and brought the donkey and the colt, and laid their coats on them; and He sat on the coats.* [8] *Most of the crowd spread their coats in the road, and others were cutting branches from the trees and spreading them in the road.* [9] *The crowds going ahead of Him, and those who followed, were shouting, "Hosanna to the Son of David; blessed is He who comes in the name of the Lord; Hosanna in the highest!"* [10] *When He had entered Jerusalem, all the city was stirred, saying, "Who is this?"* [11] *And the crowds were saying, "This is the prophet Jesus, from Nazareth in Galilee."*

The quote from the Messianic Psalm 118 along with the crowd's cries of *"Hosanna to the Son of David!"* acknowledged Jesus Christ as the Messiah. The teachers of the Law, the Sadducees and the Pharisees, knew exactly what the people were saying. These leaders were losing power and were having none of it, whereupon they immediately confronted Him on the issue.

Matthew 21: 15-16

[15] *But when the chief priests and the scribes saw the wonderful things that He had done, and the children who were shouting in the temple, "Hosanna to the Son of David," they became indignant* [16] *and said to Him, "Do You hear what these children are saying?"*

Entry into Jerusalem by Pedro Orrente c1620

Jesus responded to their complaints; then He left. The following day when He returned to the temple, His critics confronted Him once more. This time Christ rebuked them even more harshly:

Matthew 23:27-39

[27] *"Woe to you, scribes and Pharisees, hypocrites! For you are like whitewashed tombs which on the outside appear beautiful, but inside they are full of dead men's bones and all uncleanness.* [28] *"So you, too, outwardly appear righteous to men, but inwardly you are full of hypocrisy and lawlessness.* [29] *"Woe to you, scribes and Pharisees, hypocrites! For you build the tombs of the prophets and adorn the monuments of the righteous,* [30] *and say, 'If we had been living in the days of our fathers, we would not have been partners with them in shedding the blood of the prophets.'* [31] *"So you testify against yourselves, that you are sons of those who murdered the prophets.* [32] *"Fill up, then, the measure of the guilt of your fathers.* [33] *"You serpents, you brood of vipers, how will you escape the sentence of hell?* [34] *Therefore, behold, I am sending you prophets and wise men and scribes; some of them you will kill and crucify, and some of them you will scourge in your synagogues, and persecute from city to city,* [35] *so that upon you may fall the guilt of all the righteous blood shed on earth, from the blood of righteous Abel to the blood of Zechariah, the son of Berechiah, whom you murdered between the temple and the altar.* [36] *"Truly I say to you, all these things will come upon this generation.*

[37] *"Jerusalem, Jerusalem, who kills the prophets and stones those who are sent to her! How often I wanted to gather your children together, the way a hen gathers her chicks under her wings, and you were unwilling.* [38] *"Behold, your house is being left to you desolate!* [39] *"For I say to you, from now on you will not see Me until you say, 'Blessed is He who comes in the name of the Lord!'"*

Any question that Jesus was not aware that He was the Messiah should be dispelled by the previous exchanges. He not only knew what the crowd was saying but he also re-quoted it later, during Passover with His disciples, when He introduced the New Covenant, which gave all prior events a heightened meaning.

The Sign Over the Door

According to scripture, the innocent lamb's blood was applied to the sill, beam or ledge over the door and to the doorposts on each side. Hebrew tradition in the Talmud and elsewhere tells us that it was applied with a hyssop branch dipped in a small container of blood placed at the door's base.

Exodus 12:7
[7] *'Moreover, they shall take some of the blood and put it on the two doorposts and on the lintel of the houses in which they eat.*

THE MARKING ON THE DOOR

If we were standing away from the door to which the blood was applied, it might very well appear as in the preceding illustration. Yet, if we look for a pattern, it is there and you can see it—applied over the door. It's a symbol of salvation from sin and death, as was the cross on which Jesus was crucified.

THE MAKING OF A CROSS – IS IT BY COINCIDENCE?

Summary

It is more than coincidence that those of the Jewish faith who rejected Jesus continue to wait for the coming of the Messiah. It is what is meant during the Passover service when they say, *"Baruch ha'ba b'shem Adonai. Blessed is He who comes in the name of the Lord."* The phrase is a repeat of Psalm 118—and Christ's prophecy.

Passover has been observed for over four thousand years. The event was given special meaning by Jesus' instructions to eat the bread and drink the wine in memory of His sacrificial death on the cross. Although many centuries have passed, the Jewish Passover of ancient times through today continues to point to Yahshua (Jesus) as the Messiah and as our salvation. For these and other reasons, Passover should hold an important purpose for the Christian.

In the chapters that follow and within the Seder service, we will discover and discuss even greater evidence of Jesus Christ that exists in the Passover.

Antoni Ciseri's depiction of Pontius Pilate presenting a scourged Christ to the people – 1871 (Behold the man!).

CHAPTER 5
A PASSOVER SCRIPT
"THE PERFORMANCE BLUEPRINT"

"The heart of man plans his way, but the Lord establishes his steps."
Proverbs 16:9

One needs a blueprint to build a house, a school, or even a car. Likewise, a plan is required to conduct a Seder successfully. This is true whether it is a home Seder or one presented in a church or other organization. The blueprint for a Seder is a "script," and one is furnished in Appendix A. It lays out every detail for each part of the service. In the home, the leader might be the father; but in the church, it might be the minister or another selected person.

Before delving into the Passover script, it is essential to understand the order of the service along with the nature of a Passover Seder.

What Is a Seder?

A Passover Seder is a part of the Passover celebration that is held in a home or in a larger group setting. It consists of a ceremony and a meal and is typically observed on the first night of Passover (Jewish tradition also provides for the Seder to be held on the second night if one cannot attend the first night). Whether celebrated on the first or second night, the Seder concludes with a dinner, which is considered a part of the service. Each partaker of the service uses a book called a Haggadah to lead as well as follow along in the service. Haggadah is a Hebrew word that means "the telling"; hence, the name of this book, which contains instructions for the Seder, the blessings, and the Passover story itself.

The word *Seder* means "the order" in Hebrew. It comes from the fact that there are fifteen parts to the order of the Seder service, including the dinner.

The following outline briefly describes each of the fifteen components of a Passover Seder, but to remain, authentic, each segment should be observed, whether in a home or group setting. A more detailed explanation of the components is contained in subsequent chapters and within Appendix A—Passover Script.

Parts of a Passover Seder

Chapter 4 provided a brief explanation of the historical order of the Passover Seder; however, the following adds to that explanation, offering the traditional names for each segment of the service along with further clarification.

1. **The Kiddush** (Sanctification)—During this segment of the service, each partaker's cup is filled with wine or grape juice. The Kiddush is first recited aloud, followed by drinking the cup.

2. **The Ur'chatz** (Washing of the Hands)—Water poured over the hands signifies a ritual purification. Traditionally, a pitcher is used, and water is poured first over the right hand, then the left.

3. **The Karpas** (Eating of the Green Vegetable)—A vegetable such as parsley, lettuce or cucumber is dipped in salt water and eaten. The salt water represents the tears the Hebrews shed during their years of Egyptian captivity.

4. **The Yachatz** (Breaking the Matzah)—A plate containing three *matzot* (the plural of *matzah*) is on every Seder table. The three are part of the ritual service, although there are other matzot available for the dinner itself. At this point in the service, the leader removes the middle matzah and breaks it in half. The smaller of the two pieces is placed between the two matzot. The larger portion is named the Afikomen, which is hidden so that children may later try to find it.

5. **The Matzot** (This is a blessing of the matzah)—At this point, a blessing is said for the matzah followed by the reading of the commandment for eating the matzah, as guided by the leader of the Seder.

6. **The Matzah**—Attendees eat their matzah.

7. **The Maror** (Bitter Herbs)—The herbs are usually a root vegetable such as horseradish, made into a prepared paste. A small amount is placed on a piece of matzah and eaten.

8. **The Korech** (The Hallel Sandwich)—Attendees, directed by the Leader, prepare a "Hallel Sandwich" by putting maror and charoset (a sweet, dark-colored paste made of fruits and nuts) between two pieces of matzah. Afterward, the sandwich is eaten.

9. **The Rachtzah** (Second Washing of the Hands)—Attendees rewash their hands, this time saying the appropriate blessing from the Haggadah.

10. **The Shulchan Orech** (The Dinner)—At this point, dinner is served, and the festive meal begins. The dishes served are Jewish and may consist of such items as matzah ball soup,

lamb, Matbucha Salad, chicken, and eggplant. Dessert often includes ice cream or flourless pastries.

11. **The Maggid** (The Telling of the Passover Story)—During this segment, the leader, accompanied at times by the participants, recites the story of the Exodus. The youngest member at the table sits to the right of the leader and begins by asking four questions. Each query becomes a variant of "Why is this night different from all others?" The leader and participants take turns in answering each of the questions. Afterward, four types of children are described (the wise, the wicked, the simple and the shy). This section of the service ends when the second cup of wine is poured. The leader recites the ten plagues that struck Egypt, and as he names each one, all participants dip their little finger into their wine and remove a drop. At this point, the leader also discusses the various symbols that appear on the Seder plate before the drinking the second cup.

12. **The Tsafon** (Eating of the Afikomen)—After the meal, the attendees eat the Afikomen, which was hidden at the beginning the service but is "discovered" by the children at this point of the Seder. The leader provides the explanation from his Haggadah for the symbolic meaning of the act.

13. **The Barech** (The Third Cup)—A third cup is poured, and the appropriate blessing from the Haggadah is recited, followed by drinking the wine. The pouring of the fourth cup of wine follows this. The leader explains that this portion is for the prophet Elijah. A door is opened so that the prophet if he returns, may enter the home or room.

14. **The Hallel** (Songs of Praise)—The leader explains, as Christ did, that for those who had understanding, John the Baptist was the return of Elijah (who made way for the coming Messiah). Since Elijah has already returned, the door is closed. At this point, everyone sings songs of praise to God before drinking the fourth and final cup of wine.

15. **The Nirtzah** (Conclusion of the Seder)—The Seder Service is now officially over, so one final blessing is said. This one always includes the hope that next year the Passover will

be celebrated in Israel. For the Christian, the expression is the same except that "next year" will be in the New Jerusalem spoken of by John in the Book of Revelation.

Asking the Four Questions

A Script is a Blueprint

A script is a written work by a playwright, screenwriter or theatrical presenter for a performance presentation (be it stage, film or theatre). One cannot effectively stage a play, make a movie or mount a production without written instructions laying out precisely what those involved will be doing. That blueprint, the script, is the structural backbone of any production.

Scripts can be original works or adaptations from existing pieces of writing. In them, the movement, actions, expression and dialogues of the characters are provided. They are called by various names:

- A script for a film is known as a screenplay.

- A script for television is known as a teleplay.
- A script for theatre or performance is generally referred to as a script.

Script Performance Responsibilities:

Performance presentations carry specific task assignments for the leaders. The following table summarizes the more common positions (these are amplified in Chapter 7).

Passover Performance Leadership Positions

A Producer has overall responsibility for the Passover production. He or she oversees all aspects of mounting the service program and is responsible for the financial and managerial functions of the program. As such, bring on board other key personnel such as the director.

The Director is responsible for the "stage" performance, lighting, sound, etc. In other words, the Director is the "parent of the set."

Committees and Workgroups carry out the tasks required for conducting a successful Passover.

> **Food Service** members are responsible for the "dinner" portion of the Passover.

These selected Passover leaders should thoroughly familiarize themselves with the Christian Passover Script that will be used in the Seder (a *Haggadah*). There are many Haggadot available, but not all are accurate, and even fewer are prepared for the Christian. As part of its mission, Bay Area Christian Publishing carries a Haggadah that is based upon the earliest available material. It is fully illustrated and contains additional documentation and biblical references with the Christian in mind. A copy is provided in Appendix A. Whether you decide to use this one or another, an initial group reading is recommended so that all become collectively familiar with what will transpire on Passover.

You may want to acquire a *Haggadah Leader's Handbook* for use by your group's director or by the leader in a home-based Passover. Its large size, additional stage directions, and illustrations make it extremely useful for both the Passover director and the Seder leader. But, if you are not involved in doing the Passover, you shouldn't need one. The handbook is a parallel Haggadah, but it includes further instructions and illustrations for the person conducting the Passover.

You will need individual copies of the Christian Passover Haggadah for each attendee, to follow the service and to take home for future reference. The publishing company leaves a space where your church name may be imprinted if you want. Attendees may keep these small booklets for a very long time.

None of the publications—the script, *Haggadah* or *Leader's Handbook*—is expensive, and either one or all may be ordered in small or large quantities from the following:

Bay Area Christian Publishing
14450 Old Galveston Road
Webster, Texas 77598
(281) 480-5683

In Summary

A script is a blueprint that is an essential part of any performance. The Passover script* in Appendix was taken from the most ancient sources available. Its luminosity is that it permits the Passover Service to clearly demonstrate that Jesus Christ's coming was foretold in this most ancient of  feasts. For that reason, I strongly recommend that it be followed, so as not to vary from tradition. I am also aware that there are many versions of the Haggadah in current use and that some Christian churches have developed their own versions. Yet, there is a great deal to be said for a "Passover Service" that observes Passover in the manner of the ancient Hebrews.

*NOTE

APPENDIX A contains a complete Seder script. A quick reading of the Passover script at this point will significantly enhance your understanding for the remainder of this book.

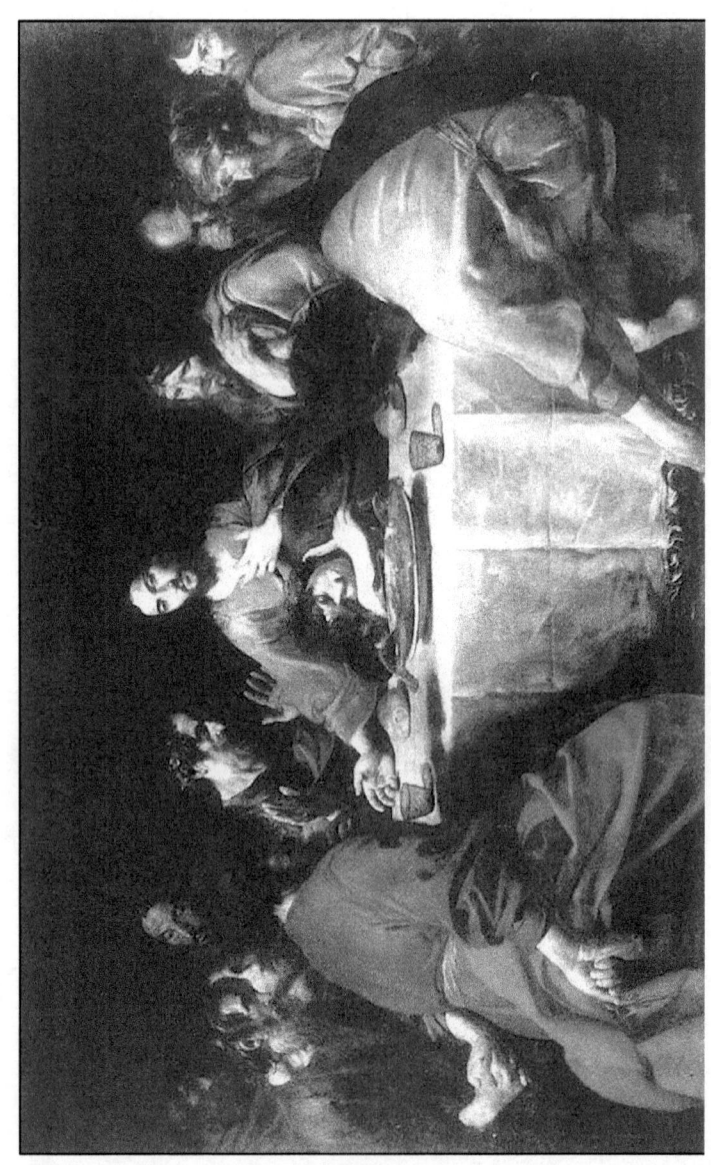

THE LAST SUPPER PAINTED BY
Valentin de Boulogne – 1625 AD

CHAPTER 6
PLANNING FOR A PASSOVER

[17] 𝔑ow on the first day of 𝔘nleavened 𝔅read the disciples came to 𝔍esus and asked, "𝔚here do 𝔜ou want us to prepare for 𝔜ou to eat the 𝔓assover?"
𝔐atthew 26:7

When the great military leader Alexander the Great was asked his secret for successful conquest, he replied with one word, "planning." He spoke a lesson for us all. This chapter provides considerable detail about planning for a Seder service that should greatly help you in preparing for yours.

STEP ONE: FIND THE CORRECT
DATE FOR PASSOVER

In the modern era, Passover begins on day 15 of the Hebrew month of Nisan and continues for eight days. On our Gregorian calendar, this falls in either March or April. Initially, Passover followed the ancient Hebrew way of marking the days. Then, a day began at sunset and ended at the same  time the next day. The celebration of Passover would start at twilight and was followed the next evening by the Feast of Unleavened Bread, which would continue for seven more days.[1]

---

[1] Leviticus 23:6

The first Passover occurred on the exact date that God decreed, which was the 14th day of Nisan. The event was so powerful that the Jewish calendar was transformed forever. The month of commemoration made Nisan the first month of the Hebrew liturgical year from that time onward.

Thutmoses III
Date of Reign: 1485 - 1431 BC
Probable Pharaoh of the Exodus
Biblical Date of the Exodus -1446 BC

Because it is a date set by God, many scholars believe that Christians should avoid falling into the non-biblical trap of placing an artificial date for Passover; however, there is nothing wrong with the time as established by the Lord in the Book of Leviticus.

Leviticus 23:5-8
[5] *'In the first month, on the fourteenth day of the month at twilight is the Lord's Passover.* [6] *'Then on the fifteenth day of the same month there is the Feast of Unleavened Bread to the LORD; for seven days you shall eat unleavened bread.* [7] *'On the first day you shall have a holy convocation; you shall not do any laborious work.* [8] *'But for seven days you shall present an offering by fire to the Lord. On the seventh day is a holy convocation; you shall not do any laborious work.' "*

We know that the original event began in the evening and at midnight as the Lord struck down all the firstborn of those who had not followed His directions. On that night Pharaoh summoned Moses and said, "Rise up, get out from among my people, both you and the sons of Israel; and go, worship the Lord, as you have said." 2 Before sunrise, the Hebrews had left with God directing them toward the Red Sea.

Traditionally, observant Jews living outside Israel conduct their Seder Services on the evenings of the 14th or 15th day of Nisan. Christians who celebrate Passover will usually do so on the 1st day. However, it isn't incorrect to observe the feast on the 2nd day. The dates correspond to late March or April in our Gregorian calendar. It is a spring festival, so the 14th or 15th of Nisan always begins on the night of a full moon following something called a northern vernal equinox. Don't panic. An Equinox is an astronomical event that occurs only twice a year. One is around March 20 and the other near September 22. The Equinox happens when the plane of the earth's equator passes the center of the sun, at which time the tilt of the earth's axis is inclined neither away from nor towards the sun.

The name "equinox" is taken from the Latin word "aequus" meaning equal and nox, denoting night. Equinox is used in a

---

2 Exodus 12:31

broader term to signify the date when such a celestial passage occurs. The Vernal Equinox refers to the "spring" (March or April) time in which an event transpires. To ensure that Passover did not start before spring, the ancient Hebrews held that the first day of Nisan would not begin until the barley was ripe, this being their test for the onset of spring.3 If the grain wasn't mature or something else indicated that spring hadn't arrived, an additional month called Adar II would be inserted into the calendar. Fortunately for us, since the 4th century, the date has been fixed mathematically.4

Passover and Easter are two crucial holidays on the Christian calendar. Frequently, both events fall near each other. This can cause apoplexy in church leadership who may become gravely concerned that celebrating one event will lower attendance at the other (usually a Good Friday Service). Let me state categorically, having done many Passover Services in weeks where Good Friday services were held, that it will not. In fact, you will soon discover that a Passover always stimulates interest and turnout in the Easter services. Let me provide another example. It is well-known within the film industry that the more films there are in the marketplace, the higher the theatrical attendance. Ancillary to that, the more successful a movie is, the larger the audiences are for other films. Likewise, the more church activities there are, the greater the overall church attendance will be. In short, "...not to worry."

The Simple Way to Find the Correct Day

---

3 The barley had to be "eared` out" (ripe) in order to have a wave-sheaf offering of the first fruits according to the Law. Jones, Stephen (1996). Secrets of Time. This also presupposes that the cycle is based on the northern hemisphere seasons.

4 "In the fourth century, ... the patriarch Hillel II ... made public the system of calendar calculation which up to then had been a closely guarded secret. It had been used in the past only to check the observations and testimonies of witnesses, and to determine the beginning of the spring season." - Spier 1952, p. 21.

If you will merely Google, "When is Passover for (insert the year)?" you will be transported to a current website that lists the dates. One such site may be found at Infoplease.com (http://www.infoplease.com/). You can also pick up the phone and call your local synagogue. In the meantime, here is a table for a decade of Passover dates:

A DECADE OF PASSOVER DATES

Fri	April 19	2019	First day of Passover
Wen	April 8	2020	First day of Passover
Sat	March 27	2021	First day of Passover
Fri	April 15	2022	First day of Passover
Thu	April 5	2023	First day of Passover
Tue	April 22	2024	First day of Passover
Sat	April 12	2025	First day of Passover
Thu	April 2	2026	First day of Passover
Thu	April 22	2027	First day of Passover
Tue	April 11	2028	First day of Passover

For informational purposes, a Hebrew calendar is provided on the following page, which also displays other dates for the other festivals (the Lord's appointed times).

STEP TWO: DETERMINE THE BUDGET

As is often said, nothing is free. You must work out your Passover budget—in other words, how much money is required to conduct the Seder service and how much will you realistically have. This includes budgeting for food, supplies, music, sets, performance activities and promotion. Start by making a master, sortable list of everything you will need. Use a Microsoft Excel or Apple Numbers type spreadsheet, or you can do it the old-fashioned way with paper and pencil. However, the computerized version is far more accessible.

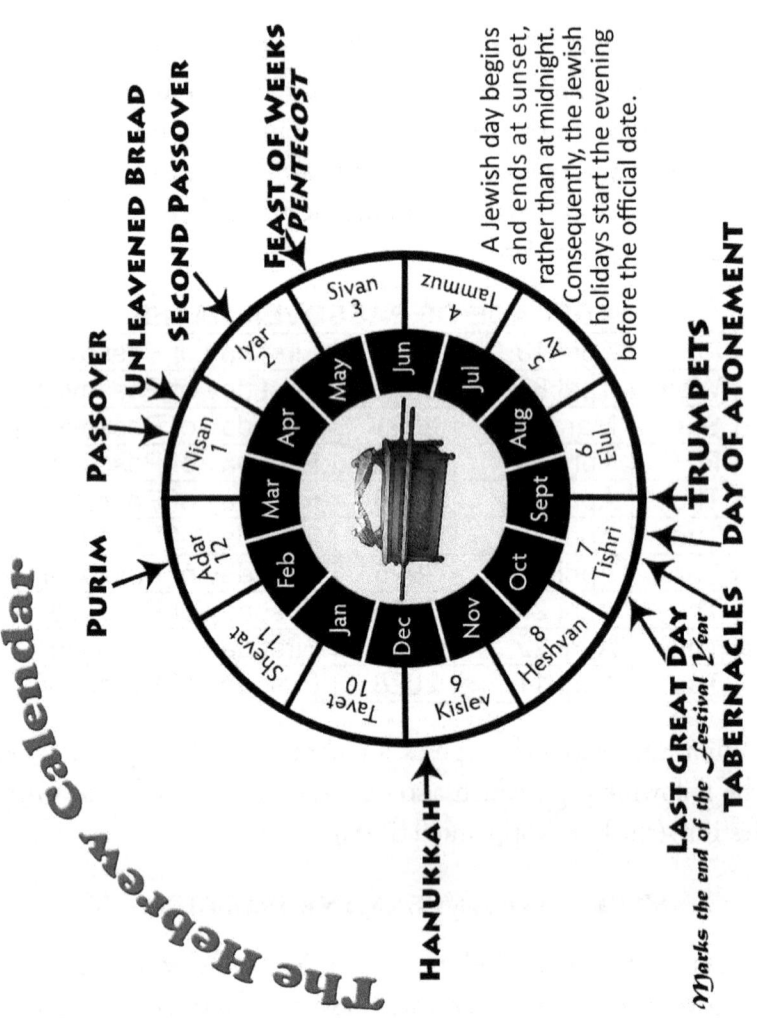

The Hebrew Calendar

PURIM

PASSOVER

UNLEAVENED BREAD

SECOND PASSOVER

FEAST OF WEEKS
PENTECOST

A Jewish day begins and ends at sunset, rather than at midnight. Consequently, the Jewish holidays start the evening before the official date.

TRUMPETS
DAY OF ATONEMENT

LAST GREAT DAY
Marks the end of the Festival Year
TABERNACLES

HANUKKAH

Nisan 1 — Apr — Mar
Iyar 2 — May — Feb
Sivan 3 — Jun — Jan
Tammuz 4 — Jul — Dec
Av 5 — Aug — Nov
Elul 6 — Sept — Oct
Tishri 7 — Oct — Sept
Heshvan 8 — Nov — Aug
Kislev 9 — Dec — Jul
Tevet 10 — Jan — Jun
Shevat 11 — Feb — May
Adar 12 — Mar — Apr

Note: The Jewish calendar date begins at sunset of the night before. Thus, all holiday rituals begin at twilight on the secular dates listed, with the day following becoming the first full day of the holiday. Therefore, the first Passover Seder is held on the evening of the first date listed. The Jewish calendar dates conclude at nightfall.

Assign each item to a category that is overseen by a committee, so that no detail "falls through the cracks." Imagine that you are preparing the meal on the day of Passover. The food committee is cooking; the service area committee is setting the tables and chairs. The service area chair asks the food committee for the paper plates and eating utensils. But, nothing is there because each committee thought the other was doing the purchasing. A matrix list is crucial for everything that needs to be bought and done.

The budget will vary from year to year, but the first year will be the more expensive if you choose to purchase specific Passover items that are needed. Afterward, they can be reused from year to year

Let's begin by discussing and analyzing the most significant cost, that of the food. Types of foods needed are considered in future chapters.

The Food Budget

No matter how you formulate your plans, the first step is to make a list of all food items. Determine the entrees, sides, drinks, and desserts. Decide if you will offer a minimal serving of lamb for the "service" or a full portion for each person. Determine whether you will only provide authentic Jewish recipes or have some alternative food (perhaps for the children). Add in the lamb, matzah, sop, bitter herbs, and wine along with any unique tableware for serving these essential items. Then decide how you will provide the food (see below). How you do it, will drive the budget. If your Passover event needs to pay for itself (i.e., is not supplemented by the church or a benefactor), then you will need to have the total cost calculated to estimate the ticket price. If the church or individuals will underwrite the event, they will likely want a reasonable estimate for each option. Potluck is also an alternative but, you will need to provide recipes in most cases.

Without exception, serving traditional Jewish foods on Passover by far exceeds the usual food fare. It lends authenticity to the service and provides instruction to all who attend.

The three ways you can handle food are discussed below: potluck, catering, or preparation at the church facility. The latter has been the most successful for our church. Pot "luck" is just that; we were lucky to get authentic dishes in and on time. Catering can be very expensive unless you can get a "deal". Of course, you could always consider a combination of ways if it works out better for you that way.

Potluck

Having attendees bring "Jewish" dishes saves costs, but it is not easy. Few people (1) known how to cook Jewish food or (2) much less know what Passover foods to bring. This means you must assign the recipes and pray. Pray that they get it right, and pray that you end up with a variety of Jewish dishes and enough food. The food committee will have to run logistics to warm the dishes and handle late-arriving food. Finally, you will be shocked at the number of recipe-variances that do arrive. You will soon question whether your handout recipes were read or not. But you do save on food costs. You must also budget for warmers, containers, servers, etc. It is often impractical to "farm out" items that must be set up ahead of time (lamb, wine, grape juice, unleavened bread). However, if the dollars saved are necessary for you to conduct your Passover, consider potluck.

Now, if you are conducting Passover in your home then either way—potluck or central preparation—will work. In this instance, you are probably planning on absorbing the costs anyway.

Catering

Your food committee can research and compare catering costs, which could be considerably costlier than the other two options. Consider your target attendee audience when analyzing this option. Catering can push the event to be cost prohibitive for some families. Again, the same items that are needed ahead of time for setup cannot be easily catered.

Central Preparation

With central preparation of food, you calculate the costs and then pass them on to the consumer. Most of the time, attendees prefer to pay rather than struggle with the preparing and transporting of food dishes.

Gather members of your Food Committee (next chapter) and put them to work on determining the costs. You can find specials on lamb and other foods. There have also been times when a considerable amount of money is saved by buying a whole lamb. Some stores will give discounts if asked.

Importantly, staff your food committee with those who know how to cook. Never hesitate to ask a professional chef to give you advice or, for that matter, help. You will, of course, thank him or her by placing their names in the bulletin under the heading of

"Thanks." Fortunately, our church had the assistance of Jason Chaney, a Culinary Institute of America graduate and a former chef at one of Houston's top ten restaurants. He was of immense help in supplying specific details regarding budgeting and recipes for Passover in this book (Chapters 12-13). Jason has been the Executive Chef for many Passover Services, and his consistency in quality has brought our Seder Services considerable praise, and by extension, increased attendance the following year. However, you don't have to have a professional chef. Most churches have excellent cooks. Use them.

It is easier if the food can be prepared centrally, and many churches have cooking facilities that are designed to do just that. But whether you are going potluck or centralizing your cooking efforts, lay out your recipes, determine the costs of food, and then budget accordingly.

The Stage-Set and Service Area Budget

You will require some sort of stage-setting along with your table placement. It may be elaborate, or it may be economical. It depends upon you. The drawing on the adjacent page and photograph on the following one display a rather simple setting for a service conducted at a medium-sized church. In later chapters, stage sets will be discussed in more detail.

The Printing Budget

Even when printing is done internally by the church or organization, there are always cost assignments. Publication expenses for Passover include costs for printing tickets (you will need them), flyers and bulletins. There are also costs for printing the evening's program. It is cheaper and easier to purchase your Haggadot (the plural form of Haggadah) than to publish them (you avoid copyright issues).

The Stage and Audio Budget:

There may be costs for lighting and sound. These must be incorporated into your planning. They might include the following:

- **Music** —printed music, scores, background tapes, musicians
- **Recording media** if you are video-copying your Passover Seder, something I recommend for historical purposes. Copies can be sold to benefit the church.
- **Backdrops**
- **On stage props** such as a menorah (if you would like one) and candles
- **Expendables** such as lighting gels and bulbs
- **Costume and Makeup** —even those costumes made in-house require fabric and sewing materials
- **Lighting and audio expendables** include lighting gels, audio filters, and electrical fuses.
- **Miscellaneous Costs** are expenses that you have not thought of, much less planned for. Typically, a 10% overage-estimate will cover them.

PLAN YOUR ORGANIZING EFFORTS

Organizing is an integral part of planning. Getting your activities organized is not tricky, but you will be surprised at how often it is not done. When done, it is often haphazard and makeshift, neither of which leads to success. Organizing is so important that it gets its own chapter—the one that follows next.

Summary

Plan and then commit your plan to writing. A necessary part of the project is the budget. Before actually budgeting, review the rest of this book, because there is a considerable amount of material that will aid you in your budget development.

Once you are ready, lay out your plan in as much detail as you can muster. The more time spent in planning, the higher your degree of success will be, and the fewer problems you will encounter. Also, by writing up the plan, you leave a legacy for the Passovers that follow. This is no small deal, and those who take leadership positions in the years to come will be extremely appreciative of your efforts.

A simple set arrangement of Passover. Notice how the tables are staggered in such a way that all attendees have a clear sightline for the stage. Also, seating is at one end of the table only. This keeps the seat's occupant from having to turn and twist continually.

RECOMMENDATION

Please consider providing each member of your Passover Staff (or the Committee Heads), a copy of this book. Besides being a lovely thing to do for volunteers who are getting ready to work very very hard, it helps each person understand the overall Seder and their role in its success.

Copies are available from:

WestBow Press, *a division of Thomas Nelson & Zondervan*
https://www.westbowpress.com/Bookstore/BookHome.aspx
1.866.928.1240

CHAPTER 7
ORGANIZING FOR PASSOVER

²¹ *"Furthermore, you shall select out of all the people able men who fear God, men of truth, those who hate dishonest gain; and you shall place these*  *over them as leaders of thousands, of hundreds, of fifties and of tens.* ²² *"Let them judge the people at all times; and let it be that every major dispute they will bring to you, but every minor dispute they themselves will judge. So, it will be easier for you, and they will bear the burden with you.*

Exodus 18:21-22

Organizing is a management process centered on the concepts of specialization and division of labor. Division of labor occurs when a specific responsibility is assigned to another (or others). Specialization happens when the accountability for a task is attached to a designated person or group best able to carry out the job. They may or may not be an expert, but they do have a responsibility to accomplish the assigned task. Organizing and division of labor are what Jethro referred to in Exodus 18:21-22 (above) when he advised Moses in the wilderness.

The organization process divides an entire work into manageable units and assigns each unit's tasks to individuals so that the overall objectives are achievable. This is smart!

Organize First!

Conducting a Passover, even for a medium or small-size congregation, is a significant effort but one made far more straightforward if you organize first. Performance events require structure for support, and a Passover Seder is no different. An organizational structure provides direction along with opportunities for congregational participation. The more volunteers who are invested in the production, the more successful it will be.

The number of committee volunteers that are used depends upon the size of the Seder you choose to do, and your personal or organizational requirements. Each committee will require a committee head to be accountable for the assignments and activities for that committee. The old saying, "Everyone can't be the boss!" is entirely accurate and even more so in the kinds of organizational activities requiring volunteers.

Usefully involving more people generates interest and excitement, which leads to higher attendance and overall success of the event. Using participants from outside the congregation is also a fruitful outreach. Over the past decades, I have occasionally found it very beneficial to seek outside help. I've never had it go badly, and frequently the church ended up with many new members. In fact, my church uses Passover as part of its outreach. It has not only worked well but has remained entirely cost-free to the church for over a quarter century.

The Passover Seder Leaders:
The Producer and the Director

A church, group or organization requires leadership at different levels; therefore, choosing effective leaders is vital. The principal leaders of a Passover service are two people, the producer, and the director. These positions should be assumed by different individuals to avoid the burnout that will most assuredly occur when the tasks are combined.

The producer has the overall responsibility for supervising and managing the entire affair, from food to performance. The position is one requiring extraordinarily good human-relations skills. Most churches must have non-paid volunteers, and these require special handling. An older person (late 40s and up) experienced in management tends to do the best job, because they are often less flappable, less excitable, and are given less flack when problems do occur.

The producer is responsible for the event and coordinates all the activities among the director, the committees and the church. The producer has the obligation for maintaining financial coordination and accountability for the occurrence. Except for the performance activity, the producer must appoint or seek volunteers as chairs for each non-performance committee and then set up and conduct periodic status meetings (frequently checking with each chair individually).

The director, on the other hand, is responsible for supervising and coordinating the overall performance segment of the event, including everything that pertains to the event's writing, staging, and performance.

It is helpful if the director has stage or media performance experience. Most churches will have at least one such individual. Sometimes, however, you may need to look elsewhere. Don't hesitate, because you will be surprised at how many from outside the church will welcome the opportunity. The performance part of the Passover does not have to be Broadway quality, but one should keep in mind that the Passover is being done with reverence for the Lord, and it should be as professional as possible. Keep your standards high and make sure that your director does the same.

The Director's Job

- Interfaces with the church management to schedule and reserve the building for rehearsals.

- Asks or appoints volunteers to fill performance committee chair positions such as the following:

  o   Staging committee
  o   Lighting and audiovisual committee
  o   Music committee
  o   Costume and makeup committee
  o   Staging and presentation committee

- Sends out a general status communication regarding his or her area of supervision.

- Schedules periodic performance committee meetings, including a final status meeting one-week before the service.

- Sets the rehearsal dates and informs the performance committee chairs.

It is essential to maintain a good working relationship between the producer and the director. There will be common areas of crossover, and each should be mindful of the other.

COMMITTEES AND WORK GROUPS

Committee Roles and Responsibilities

Orchestrating a Passover Seder is like running any significant event in that many committees must work independently for a smooth-running event. You should try and organize your committees and work groups per the work that needs to be done. By not overburdening any one group, you will be more successful in getting everything completed. Other than your central management meetings, leave it up to the committees to decide their schedules. The Producer and Director along with the Committee Chairs should keep their meetings to a minimum and set agendas to  hold the sessions focused on the tasks at hand (it helps not to bore people or use their volunteered time unwisely). If the producer and the director make a habit of publishing a schedule for their meetings, most likely their committee heads will do the same. Agendas are best when they are kept short and direct.

Let each committee chair recruit the volunteers for his or her committee. Indeed, the producer or the director may offer suggestions or help if asked. Placing the responsibility on those supervising the effort increases your odds for success.

The committee chairs selected or recruited by the producer and director should:

1. Attend meetings called by the producer or the director.
2. Call meetings as required.
3. Recruit committee volunteers that they feel are needed.
4. Follow through to make sure that all tasks are done, particularly those on the committee checklists.
5. Seek help from the producer or the director, if help is needed.
6. Provide appropriate feedback on the committee activities or problems.

Committees don't have to be large in size, just functional. They are best composed of volunteers having some knowledge in the committee's tasks. By experience, I have discovered that there are often crossover volunteers. Crossovers occur when a volunteer has an interest in working on committees other than the one to which he or she is assigned. Let them, since it is often necessary when working with smaller numbers of volunteers. Again, don't hesitate to look outside your congregation or organization to recruit volunteers if you need to.

The committees most likely needed for a medium- to large-sized Passover (150 attendees or more) are as follows:

- Management Committee
- Program Committee
- Food Committee
- Promotion and Marketing Committee
- Set Design and Stage-Setting Committee
- Lighting and Audio Visual Committee
- Music Committee
- Costume and Makeup Committee

- Staging and Presentation Committee
- Set-up/Food Service and Clean-up Committee
- Child Care Committee

The committee names are self-explanatory; however, a discussion of each follows next because it's imperative that the committees understand what is required of them in conducting a Passover. [1]

Management Committee

This small committee consists of the producer and the director. From time to time, the committee is expanded to include other committee heads. This committee interfaces with all committee chairs and other relevant church or organizational committees. Its main job...follow-up!

Program Committee

The program committee handles ticket printing and selling, designing fliers, placing pertinent information in the appropriate church and community newsletters (or other suitable electronic distribution), turning in all checks, cash or credit card receipts to the church (for deposit), and providing a status/final report for ticket sales and money spent. They are responsible for ordering the *Haggadah Leader's Handbooks*, scripts, Haggadot, and for printing the evening programs. They coordinate with the producer and authorize reimbursement to those who have purchased items for use at Passover. During ticket sales, the committee will determine how many children will require child care and recruit an

---

[1] The committees' titles are descriptive only, and the producer and the director may change them if they wish.

appropriate number of adults or mature teens for nursery duty. The program committee interfaces with the producer, the director, and the management committee to report the expected attendance, whatever it may be. They may also interface with the music committee and the staging committee.

Food Committee

The food committee sees that all the necessary foods are bought, prepared, served, and after the service, cleaned up. The food committee chooses a menu that includes lamb and other appropriate Jewish side dishes, including dessert and drinks. They make sure that any unique items for the Seder Plate are acquired, along with the grape juice or wine used during the program, the *Charoset (the fruit and nut paste)*, the unleavened bread, and all associated paper goods and candles. The food committee interfaces with the set-up/clean-up committee to coordinate where the food service tables are located, as well as times to set out the Seder Plates, drinks, and food before and during the Passover event. The food committee disposes of leftover food, and the clean-up committee then takes over with the final cleaning of the dishes and facilities.

Promotion and Marketing Committee

The promotion and marketing committee is responsible for all the marketing efforts that may be required to "fill the seats." They are responsible for drafting advertising for both inside and outside the church or organization. They may develop skits that explain Passover, for use in the Sunday school forum and church, or for presentation outside the church. They report directly and are responsible to the producer, but they should interface with all other committees and groups as needed.

Staging Committee

A STAGE SETTING FOR A PASSOVER SEDER

The Staging Committee sets up, takes down, and puts away the "props" for the Passover (like a stage committee for a play). The committee is responsible for designing and setting up the stage. If a live lamb were involved, this committee would oversee obtaining and caring for it as well. This committee has no responsibility for the congregational serving tables (as this is done by the set-up/clean-up committee). The Staging Committee interfaces directly with the director.

Light and Audio-Visual Committee

Adequate light placement and proper sound for both music and speech are essential to the success of a Passover service. Members of this committee must be knowledgeable in the functional areas of light and sound. Usually, those operating the light and sound systems for the Sunday-morning service are the ones "encouraged" to volunteer. Where there is a lack of expertise, it will serve you well to look elsewhere in your community. Most areas have "Little Theatres," and high schools, colleges, and universities who are often very willing to help. They need only be asked and, of course, appreciated for their efforts.

Music Committee

The music committee is responsible for all the program's music and sound. This committee selects the songs in conjunction with the director, recruits the singers, sets rehearsals for the singers, and provides and or recruits musicians. Where necessary, they obtain prerecorded background music and develop rehearsal recordings for the Passover program. The committee maintains and catalogs all hard-copy music, and then stores CDs and other albums for future years. The music committee interfaces with the director and the program and Staging Committees.

Costume and Makeup Committee

The costume and makeup committee is responsible for the design, manufacture, and storage of all costumes required for the production. The members plan and coordinate with the director for the application of makeup before the performance. They directly interface with the Set Design and Staging Committees.

Set-up/Food Service and Clean-up Committees

If there is one activity that directly impacts the morale of your volunteers, it is in the set-up and clean-up activities. The set-up and clean-up committees should be chaired by the same person to assure that items are returned to their proper place. If you have enough manpower, you can have two work crews. This removes the labor-intensive workload from your other committees who, by Passover time, are exhausted.

The work expected of these support committees should be limited to set-up and clean-up. Willing teens can typically staff these critical groups. The effect on morale cannot be measured in its importance to the entire Seder and upon future Seder's. Having these two committees will prevent the recruiting of guests and attendees for clean-up (which should never be done because it will 100% break the mood that you have worked so hard to establish). Both committees, interface with the management and food committees.

The set-up committee is responsible for the primary table and chair layout to accommodate the food serving and the guest seating arrangements. This includes recruiting help well ahead of time to do the intensive labor. Tables should be set up as far in advance as possible but not so soon that it interferes with other church activities. Set-up includes tablecloths, table items (washbasins, pitchers, menorahs, candles, filled Seder plates, and filled water glasses and pitchers). The set-up committee ensures that enough help is present to carry the prepared food to the tables during the first half of the Passover presentation.

The clean-up committee can begin work immediately after the meal and continue through the second half of the program. This committee can help carry food back to the kitchen, help with food storage, and wash dishes. This committee is also in charge of cleaning everything and putting it back where it belongs.

Child Care Committee

The childcare committee is responsible for the care of the children who attend the Passover. This includes creating a hands-on program to educate and entertain the children on the history and fundamentals of Passover. This committee also recruits teachers and helpers to present the children's program for those too young to participate with the adults. This committee may create and print a Passover activity booklet for the children who will be attending with their parents.

Summary

> **The only work that gets done is that which is inspected—not expected!**

Work committees are essential to a smooth and successful public Passover Seder event. Each Passover committee needs a committee head responsible for the tasks carried out by their committee. Each committee head is responsible for staffing his or her group. Care should be used in selecting those individuals who serve. They should have some expertise in the committee area to which they are being assigned. However, volunteers who do want to "work to learn" should be encouraged to do so. This year's learner might be next year's committee head.

CHAPTER 8
DIRECTING A PASSOVER

All these were under the direction of their father to sing in the house of the LORD, with cymbals, harps and lyres, for the service of the house of God. Asaph, Jeduthun and Heman were under the direction of the king.
1 Chronicles 25:6

This chapter is about the "art" of directing. While reading, this material is valuable if you are staging an in-home Passover, it is primarily geared for those charged with producing a Passover for a large group setting. Therefore, if you are not engaged in a church or organizational Passover, you may skip this chapter, continuing on to Chapter 9. On the other hand, if you are considering becoming a director, the following pages may be of interest. No matter whether you are a special events director or a director for stage, film, or television, a director's central role remains much the same.

A synonym for "directing" is "leading," and the leadership function has been with us for a very long time. In film and theatre, the person who oversees and orchestrates all aspects of a production is the director. The director's mission is to lead members of the performance team into realizing the director's vision or that of the studio. He or she works with groups of creative talent in lighting, acting, set design, costuming, makeup, props and other forms of stagecraft to ensure satisfactory performance.

Different directors use a wide variety of techniques and philosophies to achieve their goals. However, the director's primary role is to direct the play or performance. For that reason, it is preferable that the director has prior experience because Passover activities are very similar.

Duties of a Director

The director and the producer choose a script for a performance event, play or film. However, considering that the choice of a Passover text carries essential spiritual and theological overtones, a minister should be involved as well. As soon as the script is chosen, the director takes over.

Determining the Concept

The first thing a director does is to determine what his script is about. This is a critical aspect of directing because everything stems from this concept. In a Passover, many themes can be developed using music, dialogue, slides and the like, but not all topics carry the same weight, so the director decides which ones are to be emphasized. The choice will differ from director to director.

It takes considerable script work analysis to decide the principal themes of any written work. One useful technique is to analyze the script text in reverse. For example, if in the finale a critical issue is revealed, then read backward until you find what led to or motivated that theme. By working in this direction, essential questions are first raised in the director's mind for which he must then seek answers. Determining subtle differences will impact the final development of a Passover production.

Few people in any performance medium read a script all the way through. That may be shocking to some, but sadly, it is true. Most actors read a performance work to see how many lines of dialogue they have, just as costumers read to determine how many costumes they must make and for whom. Stuntmen read a screenplay to assess the number of fights or the number of times someone will fall off buildings. Since many fail to understand the entire script, the director must. He or she must know the text forwards and backward. When asked what this or that means, the director must know the answer, obsess over the script, research if need be, remember the Passover story as though he has experienced it firsthand, and understand the characters as well as he knows members of his family. If the director fails to have a solid vision of what the Passover is about, no one else will, either. Only at this point is the director ready to move onto casting and set design.

Casting

There are only a few acting roles in the Passover script, but they are essential. When casting these positions, the director must keep in mind the specific needs that his interpretation of the material requires. Casting can triple the amount of work you must do, or it can cut it dramatically. Do not cast according to "who you know." Instead, select the person who is best for the role. Friends will come to a director wanting to do this part or that. The director must resist those temptations—working instead to put the right actor in the proper role.

"Acting" Roles in the Christian Passover

The Priest (male): This is the senior figure in the service (referred to in some scripts as the Priestly Figure). In a home-based Passover, it will generally be the father, but in a single-parent household, it could be the mother. This role is substantial and should be filled  by a capable actor with a strong voice. He should have a good memory. While the dialogue may be read, it is much more potent if delivered as though it were being spoken for the first time. Age should be 35 or older.

The Narrator (male or female): This is the second most important role. His or her job is educating, often interfacing between the *Priest's* character and the Passover attendees. Like the *Priest*, he or she should have a good memory accompanied by a good voice. This is an acting role, and the Narrator must be engaging,  encouraging participation where participation is needed.

The Honored Wife (female): This vital role requires constant focus and attention. She must stay in character while interfacing with the "young son" during the entire performance. She leads in the ceremonial candle lighting along with the service activities of the Passover.

The Child (boy): This boy should look between the ages of seven and ten. As with the wife, the role calls for an ability to act without dialogue. There is also a critical reading of the ceremonial *Four Questions.* Children may not inherently have voices that carry well in an auditorium, sanctuary, or even a large room. Therefore, it is crucial to cast a boy whose voice rises to the challenge or else be prepared to mic him.

The Shofar Blower: The shofar instrument is blown twice during the ceremony. Someone who plays trumpet can usually blow a shofar. If you cannot find one, you may use a recording. The audience will never know the difference. The cast member handling the shofar becomes an excellent choice for giving the blessing since he is already there. This keeps the attendee's mind "in the moment" without breaking the reality of the performance.

Singers and Performers: Aside from their performance, singers and performers must be able to get on and off stage and maintain "their" characters during the performance. Naturally, they need the talent to do what is required of them. There are many lovely Jewish songs, and having them sung or played instrumentally will add to the ambiance and enjoyment of any Passover.

Good role casting is essential so don't hesitate to ask an actor to read for a role several times. Often when I have cast the lead actor, I may call others back to read with them to see if I can find a good or even better chemistry between the actors. If so, this adds immeasurably to any performance.

Casting is 90% of everything. The right actor in the proper role eliminates many of a director's artistic problems. As you cast, look for features in those who try out that embody the characters they will portray. Do not cast according to type as that will lead to shallow performances. Do strive to find parallels between the actor and the role they will play.

Set Design

The director should meet with the church or organizational volunteers who will design and build the sets. This should be done as soon as you have mastered the script. If possible, try to set up the stage before rehearsals begin. They may only be "rough-ins," but this will help.

Explain in detail to the set designers what the Passover and its performance is about. Describe your vision, talk about specific colors, images, etc., that you visualize. Be very open to their ideas.

> *Whenever I've had a choice of two ideas, and one is mine, but the other belongs to someone else, I consider this: "Is their idea as good as mine?" If so, I go with their idea and go out of my way to give them credit for it. If their idea should be better, it's a no-brainer. Go with theirs.*

The set design for Passover can be as simple as a table on a stage or incredibly elaborate with curtains, backdrops, and furniture, the budget, and availability of old sets determine the kind of staging that is employed. A very "workable set design and diagram" can be found in Chapter 5.

Rehearsals

Read-throughs. Rehearsals begin as soon as casting is over. Begin them with several general read-throughs of the script. This educates the actor and aids the director in seeing how each reads off the other and interprets their roles. Now is the time to change any interpretations that do not agree with the director's vision. Never allow actors to settle into a character they have they wrong "take" on.

Rehearsal should be thought of as a laboratory. It is a time to try different things, to experiment and repeat. It occurs as preparation for a performance. The rehearsal is a form of practicing to ensure that all details of the subsequent performance are well prepared and coordinated.

A director must come to rehearsal better prepared than his or her cast or crew. Staging problems should be pre-solved, although some experimentation can be carried out. Remember, everyone looks to the director to know what to do. Rehearsal is not the place to give actors the wrong impression.

Make the most of rehearsals. Start when you say you are going to begin, and end promptly. Encourage everyone to do their best and compliment them when they do. When you see something that is wrong, correct it before it becomes a habit. Encourage everyone to get off book (have the material memorized) as soon as possible. Establishing a creative atmosphere makes Passover rehearsals more difficult for the director, yet it becomes the most rewarding of experiences. Take the opportunity at the first read-through to give the actors a prepared rehearsal schedule. Better yet, email it to them beforehand.

After the read-through, the actors should begin work on memorization. Getting the lines down and the entrances and exits memorized can be a trying experience for everyone. Irrespective of the actor's capability, the first rehearsal off-script is scary. It is sometimes disastrous but do it as soon as you can. You cannot build your characters while the actors are still relying on their scripts. They are distracted because they are reading. Once off-script they will genuinely begin to internalize their roles and build on them.

As you progress, you will find that not everyone is needed at every rehearsal, particularly the performers, who are best off rehearsing their performances instead of listening to the actors' dialogue. It is also discouraging for anyone to attend rehearsals where they are not needed.

Blocking. Blocking a play is when you tell the actors where to stand and what to do while delivering lines. It is the first step in the regular rehearsals (after the read-through). Blocking should run smoothly and efficiently. Movement on the stage must be motivated, not random wandering. The director determines the action of each specific moment of the performance, and it begins with blocking.

STAGE DIRECTIONS

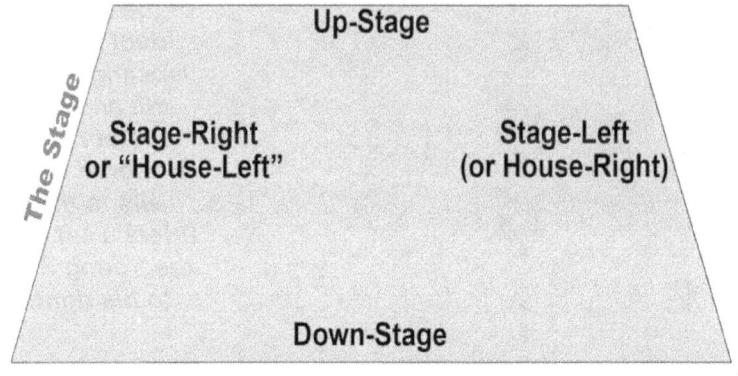

Stage directions can be confusing. The graphics for the Seder table and the stage illustrate basic stage directions common to all theatre. Upstage, downstage, stage right, and stage left are always used for blocking the positions and activities of actors. A person on stage is "down" toward the audience or up toward the backdrop, and stage-right or stage-left when facing the audience on stage. House-left, house-right directions may be used for lighting and stage construction purposes.

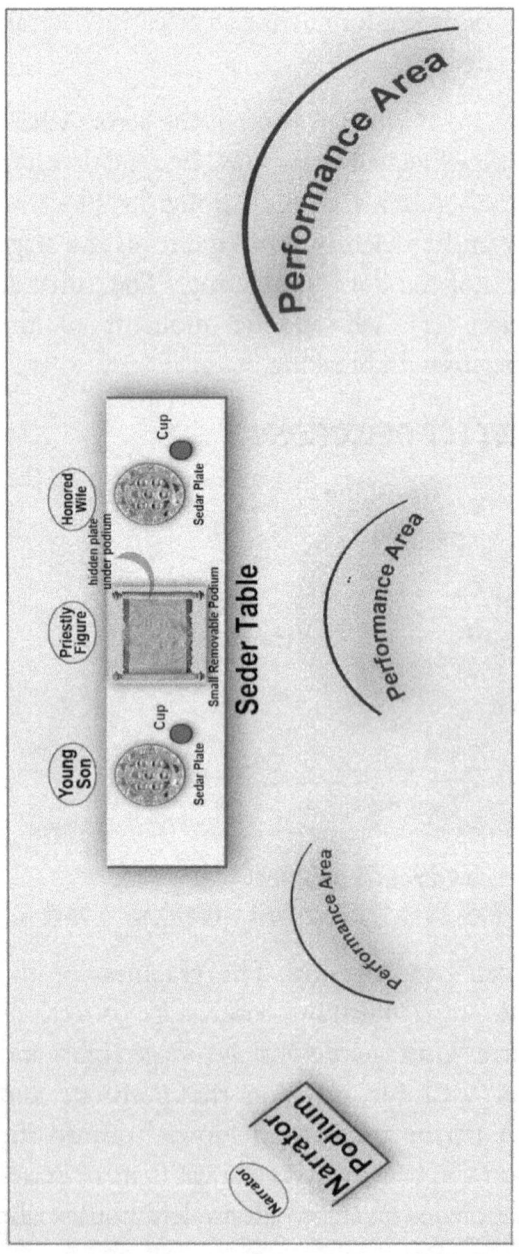

SPECIFIC STAGING AREAS AREA LAID OUT IN THE DIAGRAM TO THE RIGHT.

The positioning of the actors is evident from the labeling. As is the ancient custom, the Honored Wife sits to the Priest's left and the Young Son to his right.

The Narrator is to Stage Right so as not to intrude on the "space" created for the Seder. The various performance areas are laid out with the principal one to Stage Left.

If there is one critical rule in all of blocking, it is to keep it natural. An actor's movement should reflect what that character would or should be doing at that moment in the production. Avoid "stagey" movements as if they were the plague. Do not let actors "wander" on the stage; their movement must have a purpose.

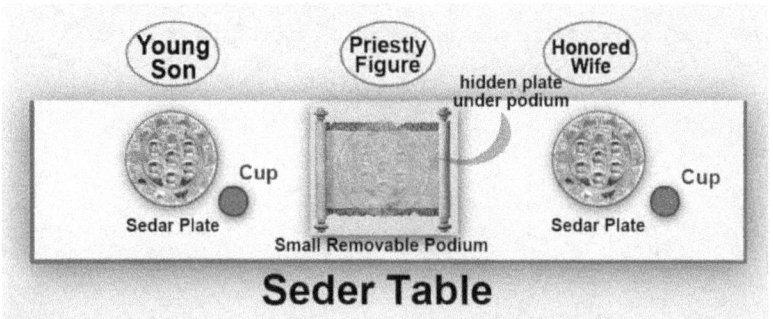

Basic staging for the Seder Table: Only one Seder Plate is required, but for observational purposes, one may use two as shown. The small podium is removable for the meal.

Dress Rehearsal

A dress rehearsal is a full-scale rehearsal where performers display every detail of the performance. Cast members wear their costumes, the sets are up, and props are used. The dress rehearsal is the final run before the actual performance.

Entrances—Exits—Props and Costumes

Entrances and exits say a lot about performance. There is nothing worse than having an audience's time wasted because a musician or an actor is late for a cue. Observe carefully to determine where your characters and performers are coming from, where they are going, what just happened, and what is happening next. Time in performances is limited, so it is crucial that it be used wisely. Missed or late cues, whether for lines or entrances and exits, are neither entertaining nor enlightening.

Props are useful tools in any performance. They should be used when needed, but only if needed. Sometimes accessories help a self-conscious actor focus on something other than fear. However, props must never be handled without a purpose in mind. Doing otherwise is awkward.

In a Passover, props are limited. Those at the Seder table are the Seder plate, certain foods, place settings, and other eating and drinking utensils. The Priest has additional props that he may use for explanations. In theatre, as in a film, you may appoint someone in the crew to care for the props —a prop-master, so to speak. Actors and performers are the ones who are blamed if the props go missing or out of place. Impress this on your talent and have them assume personal responsibility for their own props being where they are supposed to be.

A director may choose to costume those at the Seder Table or not. Because it is educational and spiritual in nature, period costuming helps. I have done it both ways and definitely come down on the side of costuming. I have found it best to have the *Narrator* character in contemporary wear but not casual. A suit and tie work nicely. You might also consider having the *Narrator* wear a Yakama and possibly a draped prayer shawl.

In costuming the priestly figure, try to get as close to the garments at the time of the Tabernacle as possible. The priest should stand out and command attention. His costume and appearance will go a long way toward achieving that goal.

In costuming the priestly figure, try to get as close to the garments at the time of the Tabernacle as possible. The priest should stand out and command attention. His costume and appearance will go a long way toward achieving that goal.

Stagecraft – Lighting, Sound, and Music

Carefully consider the illumination design for both the stage and Seder tables. Lighting is inexpensive compared to set construction and, on the cheapest of budgets, skilled lighting personnel can create a believable set that enlivens a performance and enhances the mood.

The easiest way to design lighting is to do so on paper by assigning lighting to each block of the stage. Decide which areas need increasing or decreasing illumination, the kind that is required, and when. Do the same for the table areas. Develop and determine the light cues and time them in seconds and/or minutes for the interval that they should be up. Annotate the lighting-cues in your Passover Leader's Guide or script and be sure that your lighting people have the same cues. Rehearse lighting with the actors whenever you can.

At least two weeks before the final run throughs ensure that your sound director understands all the sound cues and has prepared a sound cue sheet for the lighting crewmembers.

In times, past, audio was recorded on tape or disc and replayed during the performance. It wasn't unusual to have multiple tapes, discs, or players prepared and ready for playback. However, today's computers make sound design and placement much more accessible. The sound-director should have recorded all the sounds needed and have them programmed in sequence and ready for playback. When the recording has been done correctly, an audience will be unable to tell a recorded sound of a shofar from that of one performed live.

Music

Music is essential for Passover, particularly a group one. The director in conjunction with the music director can develop a bed of music that effectively underscores and accents dialogue, creating more interest and enlivening the performance.

Jewish music has evolved over time throughout the long course of Jewish history such that their spiritual songs and refrains are familiar in Jewish services throughout the world. The rhythm and sound of the music vary greatly depending upon the composer and the time in which the piece was written. One of the best sources for good sounding authentic Jewish music is from the Zola Levitt Ministries, located in Dallas, Texas. Visit his online store at: http://store.levitt.com/music.Another online site is the Judica Web Store at: https://www.judaicawebstore.com/.

Select an appropriate number of live performances using your church's musicians or perhaps talent from outside your group. They may not know any Jewish pieces of music, but they will know how to learn them.

If you are using the Passover script from Bay Area Christian Publishing, you will find suggested music placement within the script and the Leader's Handbook.

Otherwise, it is something you can decide according to your need.

Watch the Budget

Performances cost money. Such expenses as set-construction, rentals, costumes, and makeup can quickly mount up. Although the producer is responsible for the funds and budget, artistic choices of a director must fit within that budget.

Maintain the Mood

No curtain calls follow the Passover service. This is a celebration of what the Lord has done and not the producer, the director, the talent, the crew or the food personnel. A thank you by the narrator may be in order, but the onstage actors should

remain in character throughout the Seder (before, during and after the service). Keep the lighting appropriate and have suitable exit music. Maintain the mood everyone has worked so hard to establish. This also applies to the end of a home-based Passover.

Directing Tips That Lead to Success

I have been a director for over 30 years, and in addition to film and television, I have had an opportunity to direct my share of theatrical and stage performances including quite a few decades of Christian church Passovers. The following represent a few directing tips that I acquired during that time:

1. Read the play several times, becoming familiar with every character, even those with nonspeaking roles.

2. The first rehearsal should be a read through. Do not worry about acting at this point. If the talent doesn't know each other, have them introduce themselves.

3. Explain that everyone is welcome to bring problems or questions to you as they pertain to the performance.

4. For all rehearsals, make sure that you understand the set design and structure. You cannot block actors without it.

5. Do not tell actors how to act; they should bring their own ideas. Do offer examples of "acting choices" if their performances do not seem right to your way of thinking. If a scene is not working, it is the director's job to adjust it.

6. In the beginning, line memorization and blocking are more important than the actual acting. Only after the lines are learned does real acting begin. Some actors may have difficulty at first, while others may not be able to do it at all. However, actors can become so familiar with their lines that they don't have to rely wholly on the written page. It is recommended that you press for memorization as much as possible.

7. Set a date when all of the lines must be memorized, and when costumes and set construction must be finished. Check on the progress as your Passover deadline draws closer.

8 Solve the problems yourself, lest you lose control. If for any reason you are having trouble with an actor, resolve the issue immediately. You can recast at any time. Over the years, I have learned that virtually all actors can learn their lines and blocking in a single weekend. They may not, but they do have the ability to do it.

9. Practice all cues until they are perfect.

10. It is a good idea during some rehearsals to sit in the audience, sound booth, or backstage to make sure that—

    a. Everything is looking and sounding as it should.

    b. The actors are opening up and are visible from every point in the audience.

    c. You can hear the actors from every point in the audience.

11. During the final rehearsals—

    a. Switch seats; do not sit in the same place. Move around.

    b. Personally check that the makeup is adequate and looks right under the lights. Do not let any actor tell you he or she isn't going to wear makeup. Everyone working under performance lighting desperately needs makeup.

    c. Watch everyone's cues to see that they are happening and at the right time.

12. Before dress rehearsal, be assured there is a way for you to personally communicate with the stage manager, the music coordinator and the sound and lighting directors. Be sure they have a way to talk with you as well.

13. During the dress rehearsal, rehearse with all the actors in costume and all the sets and props in place. Rehearse everyone, including the musicians, sound, and lighting. You will be astonished at what issues come up once everyone is in makeup. Do not panic at the outcome. It does get better.

14. Follow up on everything. It is what efficient directors do. Anything that can go wrong will, and it will go wrong during the performance.

Summary

If you have done your job as a director, you will have surrounded yourself with as creative and intelligent people as possible. Encourage them; rely on them to help you. When cast and crew share in a director's vision, they feel motivated to create and perform. They become your best resources.

Whether professional or otherwise, directing is not easy. It is the toughest job in any production. Long after others have gone home from rehearsal, the director is still there, and he is always the first one at rehearsal. The director is the visionary of the group, the leader and the one who gets blamed if the final production is terrible. All the preparation and work that goes into producing a Passover pays substantial rewards that come the night of the performance.

A Christian director must approach the job with the right heart and state of mind. Remind yourself and others that what is being done are not for self-aggrandizement but for the Lord. The attendees are those participating in the Passover; God is your audience.

Finally, there is no "I" in "theatre." There is no "I" in "team." This is not a coincidence for a theatrical production and should not be for Passover.

¹⁵Therefore be careful how you walk, not as unwise men but as wise, ¹⁶making the most of your time, because the days are evil...
Ephesians 5:15,16

CHAPTER 9
TIME MANAGEMENT
CHECKLISTS AND WORKSHEETS

Benjamin Franklin wrote, "Dost thou love life? Then do not squander time, for that is the stuff life is made of."[1] One thing is sure; time not well spent is life lost. It is not that we should live our lives by the clock, but when we have specific tasks to be done, and goals to be accomplished, it does not hurt to keep our eye on the time. Those people who make the worst use of their time are the ones who complain the loudest about the lack of it. If "time flies!" then time management can make you the pilot.

An in-home Passover and a large-group Passover have one thing in common: time consumption. It takes time to prepare for either, adequately. However, if you start by making good use of your time, you will discover that the task of conducting a Passover is made far more relaxed and even more pleasurable. Time management will help you achieve that goal.

What Is Time Management *(simplified)?*

Time management is the ability to plan and control how you spend the time in your day to effectively achieve your goals. Poor time management becomes procrastination, as well as a self-control problem. Skills involved  in managing time include planning for the future, setting goals, prioritizing tasks and monitoring where your time goes.

---

[1] Benjamin Franklin, *Poor Richard's Almanac* (1746).

Multitasking is a trendy concept today, but its usefulness is dubious. Although it may appear to be a great way to get more done in a shorter time, studies have shown that multitasking adds stress, confuses the thought processes and throws one off track.[2] [3] If multitasking isn't something that works for you, make a change in your  work routine and consider using some of the following time management techniques to become increasingly more efficient.

Develop a Schedule and Task List

Taking a few moments to develop a list of everything you need to do in a selected time-period (day, week, hour) is an excellent reminder of your workload, and it helps you remain focused on the crucial tasks at hand. Keep separate lists for what must be done and the specific time and order by which it must be accomplished.

Prioritize Time—Then Keep Track of It.

Your task list should be sorted in order of priority. Should you run out of time on that day, you can rest assured your most important jobs were done. You may want to add a few of the quicker tasks to the top of the list because it can be encouraging to

---

[2] Jessica Kleiman, "How Multitasking Hurts Your Brain (and Your Effectiveness at Work)," *Forbes*, January 15, 2013.
[3] Jim Taylor, "Technology: Myth of Multitasking," *Psychology Today*, March 30, 2011.

see some things crossed off and to know you have some of the work done. Add realistic estimates of how much time each task on your list will require. This gives you an idea of how much work you will be able to get done.

Make Up a Basic Task List

Your beginning task list for the Passover can be as simple as a scrap piece of paper with a list of errands you need to complete in that time you have. Placing the most important jobs at the top and doing those first will ensure you've completed everything that you can't afford to put off. Keeping a notepad or planner that covers a few days or a week at a time will permit you to move the less important jobs to the next day if you do run out of time.

Use Your Calendar or Planner

A detailed calendar or monthly planner is a great reminder of the upcoming tasks you'll need to work on. If you've managed to knock everything off your daily task list early, looking forward on your calendar is a great way to get ahead. Keeping an eye on the future will prevent deadlines from ever sneaking up on you, so review your schedule every day or so to make sure you aren't forgetting anything.

Group Similar Errands Together

By keeping a schedule of everything you need to do, you'll be able to quickly pick out which jobs are similar enough to get done at the same time. If you have a few things that require a specific computer program, do them all at once while you have that system open. If you need to run to the market for something, see if there's anything else on your list you'll need to pick up while you're out. Getting similar jobs done all at once will make for less work while allowing you to cross more things from your list.

Time Management Tools

Task lists and calendars are two potential time-management tools that serve as reminders of  where you should be in a day, week or month. Use them to schedule blocks of time for yourself and—where possible—for others. By keeping track of the work needing to get done, you eliminate having to remember everything. This allows you to better focus on those things that are most important.

Once you have completed one task, move on to the next. To keep from getting sidetracked, make notes of ideas that come to mind, rather than stopping everything to work on them right away.

Where possible, try to work on similar tasks in succession. This helps maintain a group's train of thought as well as your own. For example, check all the e-mails at once or get all the supplies ordered in one shot. Checklists and worksheets are among the best time-management tools. Appendix B contains some select Passover checklists used by other churches. They can prove very useful in developing your own models.

Checklists

Checklists are great time aids that reduce failure by compensating for the limits of human memory and attention. They ensure consistency and completeness in carrying out a task. A typical example is the "to do" list. A more advanced checklist could be a schedule that lays out the duties to be done by some pre-established time-period or other factors.

Checklists should not be used as a replacement for thinking or common sense, but they will go a long way in helping you become more adaptive and flexible in solving potential problems before they occur.

Setting Goals and Objectives

Operating without goals and targets is like being a captain of a ship who loses his way at sea. He doesn't know where he's going, so it makes no difference where he goes. To avoid this dilemma, set targets for yourself and others that you lead, being careful that the goals are realistic and achievable.

Setting Deadlines

Strive to complete your deadlines, and, if possible, do so ahead of time. Encourage volunteers to take ownership of their work as you do likewise. Remember to use a planner to mark the essential dates against the set deadlines.

Delegating Responsibilities

Learn to say "no" when appropriate. One cannot do everything which is why it is vital to use others. Many of the roles and responsibilities can be delegated by a participant's interest and their own abilities so that assigned tasks are finished within deadlines. Bear in mind that one who is learning something new must have more time to get it done.

Develop a habit of doing the right thing at the right time. Work done at the wrong time can be wasteful. Never waste a day on something that can be done in an hour and of course, never-ever create "make-work" for volunteers.

Summary

Time management plays a vital role in staging a Passover, and checklists become excellent tools for providing volunteers with a list of tasks and times allotted for accomplishing the work. The most straightforward worksheet should include a general to-do list setting out the assignments that need to be done. These tasks should be prioritized and numbered in the order of their importance.

Checklists and worksheets should be distributed to the committees that are staging a Passover Seder. Your first handout will be a worksheet that details roles and responsibilities. This tends to get everyone on the same track toward a successful Seder. Sometimes, it's a good idea to explain each one of them at first. Eventually, you will have many of the same volunteers each year, and this will not be as necessary.

To increase productivity and efficiency learn to use specific time management tools and techniques to keep your Passover volunteers motivated and on track. You can get as complicated as you would like with time management by using multiple computer software programs, calendars, and demanding schedules, but enabling yourself to get more work done in less time can be simpler than all of that.

Start by creating a basic schedule or task worksheet to make the best use of your time. Even if you make a short list on a scrap piece of paper of everything you need to get done in a day, this can go a long way in keeping you and your groups focused on what needs to be done. You can be creative, but be sure to indicate a priority on each item and get the most important tasks out of the way first. It is a good idea to estimate how long each job will take. This way you can decide if something should be done earlier or moved to a better time.

NOTE

Turn to APPENDIX B, which contains numerous checklists that you may adapt to your specific needs.

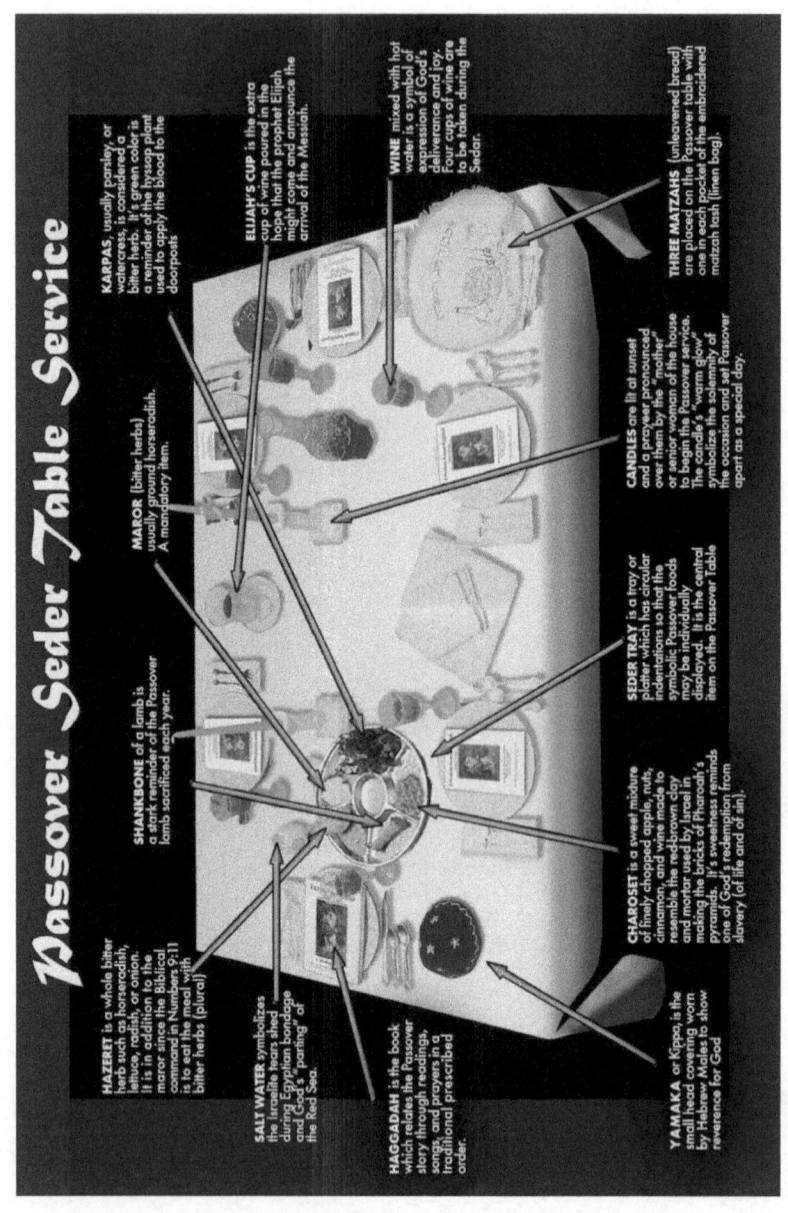

CHAPTER 10
ARRANGING THE SEDER TABLE

If you are preparing your first meal for Passover, the responsibility can feel overwhelming because of the amount of ritual and tradition from thousands of years of Jewish practice and customs. Relax and prepare to enjoy the preparation, presentation, music, and the wonderful foods. You will be pleased to know that you do not have to throw out everything that you know about cooking to observe the Passover rituals. You will be able to cook with all the vegetables that are available at your supermarket or farmer's market.

The primary purpose of a Seder is to retell the story of the Exodus, and, for the Christian, to see the enormous volume of prophecy in Passover that points to the ministry, death, and resurrection of Jesus Christ. The meal makes the "telling" more engaging, and, if scheduled right, fits seamlessly into the overall service.

The Passover is not unlike other holidays. Christmas and Thanksgiving call for certain foods, such as roast beef, turkey, and various custards. Passover, too, has its staples, such as charoset, matzah, and lamb. Brisket, potatoes, asparagus, and other vegetables may also be served. Indeed, some foods do not fit, such as pork or shellfish. Bread or desserts using yeast are not allowed. Other than a few rules, Passover presents a beautiful opportunity for a family or church meal using tasty foods from another culture. If your children are from a fast-food-hamburger-and-French-fry culture, they will be shocked. Once over it, they will enjoy the experience. Lamb prepared correctly is out of this world, and the same can be said for the many Jewish recipes for chicken, roasts, fish, and cabbage. Passover recipes include many tasty desserts as well.

How Long Should a Seder Last?

A typical Passover service runs from an hour and a half to two hours. A reasonable start time might be 6:30 or 7 p.m., with a conclusion around 9 p.m. People sometimes travel many miles to attend a Passover service, and most must work the next day. Please keep this in mind when deciding the start time and length of the service. Remember that a successful Seder is not measured by the amount of time spent reading the Haggadah, discussing the Exodus, or the length of the meal. A "great" Seder is one in which everyone has an opportunity to participate and learn. Every member of your family or group should take part in the service. It is far easier to have a "participatory" Seder when the Haggadah is more than just a story text.

Seating

In this chapter, we will use a home table setting of six to eight. Obviously, a larger group setting will have multiple tables. Therefore, instead of a single table seating eight, increase the number of tables to accommodate the number of guests. In other words, duplicate enough tables to seat the participants comfortably. However, avoid seating at locations that would require guests to turn awkwardly to view the stage.

Preparation for Passover—Searching for Leaven

Passover comes in the spring, and the Jewish housewife tackles her spring-cleaning with moral fervor. In doing so, she obeys the commands in Exodus 12:19: "'... Seven days there shall be no leaven found in your houses; for whoever eats what is leavened, that person shall be cut off from the congregation of Israel, whether he is an alien or a native of the land.'" In other words, every morsel of bread or cracker crumbs, all the baking powder, and yeast had to go. Passover became an opportunity to do a thorough cleaning.

If the cost for "getting rid" of the leaven became too expensive, then the housewife might find a Gentile friend to hold the "bag" of goods for her until after the Passover. The friend would pay a token amount, then seven days after Passover, allow the products to be redeemed for the same amount.

In ancient times, a ceremonial search for the leaven was part of the ceremony. The head of the house would usually take a child bearing a candle with him together with a feather, wooden spoon, and a cloth napkin. Together they would search the house for leaven. The housewife, knowing the order of the search, would place a few crumbs of leaven to be discovered in the last room. After the search, the man announces: "Now, I have rid my house of all leaven."

If the Passover is being held in the home, then you will be cleaning anyway. In a larger venue, cleaning occurs as well. Perhaps consider teaching the children that leaven to the Israelites was a symbol of sin. Explain that a "little sin" like a little leaven, expands and puffs up. Make clear that Passover is a time to remove sins from our lives and to do as the Hebrews did, begin again. For the Christian, God's grace through Jesus' sacrifice covers all those who believe and follow His word and commandments.

After the home or church area is cleaned, everyday dishes are put away, and unique dishes and utensils are set out. This is very much like "putting out the china" or the yuletide platters and plates during Christmas. In a Seder, certain items are explicitly used for the service (and these will be detailed later).

What to Wear?

Traditionally, attendees wore their "Sunday best" out of respect for the event (often referred to as Sunday go-to-meeting clothes). Keep in mind the setting of fine linen and lighted candles. The day is considered a Sabbath. In the present day, however, many may choose to come in attire that is more casual. If you are the sponsor of the event, you may make a choice. Frankly, my own experience has led me to err on the side of a little better dress code than usual.

About Head Coverings

To a Christian, head covering is the veiling of the head by women or men in a variety of Christian traditions. Some veil only in public worship, while others believe they should cover their heads all the time. Very few contemporary Christians, however, practice this.

Head coverings became an issue during one of the first Passovers that I was engaged in. Someone suggested that men be provided with a Yakama, but almost immediately, the discussion switched to a necessity for women, not men, to cover their heads. The debate stemmed from Paul's admonition to the Corinthians that women's heads be veiled but that if a man's head was covered, it was wrong.[1] However, a little research and study revealed that Paul was probably addressing a problem that had arisen in the Corinthian church. Ancient sources indicate that Greek women commonly participated in religious ceremonies without head

---

[1] 1 Corinthians 11:2-16

coverings. So, it seems unlikely that Paul is advising conformity to Jewish customs in which women hid their faces in public.

Use of head coverings by women was every day enough in the ancient world that we might expect Paul to make his meaning clearer if this were a requirement. Instead, Paul uses a very general Greek word for covered. One thing is certain. Paul is not advising conformity to Roman customs of his day, in which male priests usually covered their heads for ceremonies. Therefore, he is openly urging the Corinthians to observe an established tradition of the church.

In the modern era, there are several views on the practice within churches:

1. A view that the text has no applicability today, and that Paul is speaking about a "tradition" of the time.

2. The head covering is the hair ones has, therefore, women should wear (relatively) long hair.

3. The head covering is an actual physical covering, so therefore Paul's text is as applicable today as it was in in his day.

4. The head covering was a purposeful symbol in an ancient world which needs some sort of a equivalent symbol today, but not necessarily a head covering.

Styles changed over the years but the practice of head covering continued up to the early 20th century. By the 1960s in the West, the biblical method had become a tradition, so when hats fell out of style, the practice was dropped in Christian churches as well.

Since the wearing of a Yamaka in Passover is a common practice for Jewish men, I see no problem with it. It is, after all, an ancient practice. I personally view the wearing of a Yamaka as a nice touch, and it adds to the mood of a Passover whether in a home setting or a larger church one. Yamaka caps are inexpensive and easily obtained online or from your local synagogue. They come in various styles, sizes, and designs. However, costs are minimal if you select a basic white cloth or even paper one.

The 12 Steps of Passover Preparation

The following table summarizes each of the twelve steps of preparation for Passover. One might have but on average, this is what it takes.

12 STEPS IN PREPARING FOR PASSOVER

1. Invite Your Guests: Invite family and friends, of course. Keep in mind that Passover is highly educational for Christians. Consider inviting others who might benefit.

2. Do the Shopping: Prepare shopping lists of goods that you will need, especially some of the specialty items such as the kosher cakes and grains. To keep your return trips to the market at a minimum, carefully prepare a shopping list. There are more than a few components to this ritual feast, and a checklist will help you keep track of everything from the number of Haggadot required to the number of wine glasses needed.

   Add the following "must have" items to your shopping list. Explanations will follow later.

   - Horseradish
   - Charoset *(explained later)*
   - Wine
   - One Haggadah per guest
   - Candles
   - Matzah
   - Candles

2. Choose your Haggadah: This book explains the Exodus and its significance. It should also provide directions for the Passover attendees as well as their role in the responsive readings. There are many variations of the Haggadah, but I strongly recommend the version published by BACC Publishing. Furthermore, its contents are based upon the most ancient Passover references available and have stood the test of time and usage for the Christian.

3. Cleaning: activities were discussed in the earlier paragraphs of this Chapter.

4. Preparing the dinner: More on this in chapters 12 and 13, but apparently, you want to finish the cooking before guests arrive. Remember, you must not include any bread or other foods containing leaven. Typical dishes may consist of lamb, brisket, and chicken, chopped liver and green and yellow vegetables. Of course, a dessert is always welcome.

5. Prepare the matzah: Three pieces of matzah (per table) are placed in a white linen bag or cloth. I recommend a bag because these are easy to sew. Inside the bag, put a white cloth so that the pieces are not touching. It also makes it easier to remove the middle matzah later. The matzah may be baked fresh (recommended if possible) or purchased from a supermarket or bakery.

6. Prepare the Kosher grape juice or kosher wine and serving glasses: The grape juice or wine used in the service should be set apart from other drinks or wines offered. You will need a minimum of four glasses of juice/wine per attendee. I recommend using wine glasses instead of water glasses. The wine glasses contain less of the beverage, and they look nice on a table.

7. Roast a shank bone: Lamb is traditional, and these may be obtained from most meat markets. They are placed on the Seder Plate, so only one per table is required.

8. Prepare the Charoset: This is the ceremonial fruit and nut mixture which symbolizes the slave labor using bricks and mortar that the Egyptians forced upon the Jews. There is an excellent recipe in Chapter 13.

9. Prepare the bitter herbs: Two bitter herbs are used. The first is the maror, which is usually grated horseradish. The second herb called the *chazeret* is a vegetable like lettuce or radish (Romaine lettuce is an excellent choice). It's combined with the charoset and matzah to make a sandwich *(called the Koresh)*

10. Wash the ceremonial vegetables and dissolve the salt: A green vegetable such as celery or parsley may be used. The greens symbolize the season of spring (the time of Passover) and rebirth from slavery for the Jew and from sin for the Christian. During the ceremony, the vegetables will be dipped into the salt water and eaten. Small bowls are used, one per attendee.

11. Arrange the Seder Plates: Prepare one per table. There is more on preparing of the Seder Plate in Chapter 11.

12. Prepare for the arrival of guests: It isn't necessary for Christians, but you may want to consider providing the men and boys a Yamaka as they enter.

Preparing the Seder Table

Each table should be covered with an appropriate but festive tablecloth and napkins. Color varies; white linen is lovely, but so are colored cloths. Each place setting should include a plate, flatware (eating and serving utensils such as knives, forks, and spoons), a water glass, wine or kosher grape juice glass, and a Haggadah. In a home setting, you will want your leader and the narrator each to have an easy-to-read *Haggadah Leader's Handbook*, as it contains essential notes and instructions that are not in the Haggadah.

The small dishes for salt water and containers for the wine or grape juice should be conveniently placed so that everyone has access to them. One empty wine glass (the Cup of Elijah) is positioned in the middle or very end of the table for the prophet. Set a Haggadah on top of each plate. The attendee will remove it to a place of convenience when it comes time to use either it or the service items.

Place the plate holding the three pieces of matzah on the Leader's plate. In a home setting, the Seder Plate is placed conveniently near the Leader for demonstration. In a group setting, the table's Seder Plate will be situated near the center or at one end of the table. The exception will be for the "on-stage" table. There, it will be placed in front of the Priest (for ease in the demonstration).

Regarding the Matzah

Not all matzah sold in groceries or the supermarket is suitable for use at Passover. The matzah should be kosher and will be labeled as such. If the identification does not read KP or (U)P, then it is meant to be used as a snack. The packaging might also read "Kosher for Passover."

The Menorah

A menorah is a seven-branched lampstand used in the ancient desert tabernacle and in the Jerusalem temple. It is not a requirement of Passover but does add ambiance to the settings. Unknowingly, Christians often select a nine-branched menorah. This one is used only during Hanukkah, a separate Jewish celebration.

The menorah has heavy Christian symbolism connected to it. The New Testament describes a menorah as holding the "lights of the seven churches," listed as Ephesus, Smyrna, Pergamum, Thyatira, Sardis, Philadelphia, and Laodicea. Many of the letters of the New Testament are written to these bodies. The menorah's seven lamps also allude to the branches of human knowledge, represented by the six lamps inclined inward toward, and symbolically guided by, the light of God represented by the central lamp. The menorah also symbolizes the creation in six days, with the center light representing the Sabbath. It has also been said to symbolize the burning bush as seen by Moses on Mount Horeb.

For a large Passover, a sizable menorah is good. Although they can be purchased, they can also be built as the latter is less expensive. It should be placed near the leader's table where it can also be used in the candle lighting portion of the service. A single small menorah for each of the tables is quite suitable. The menorah adds light to the table and warmth and authenticity to the mood.

After the table or tables have been arranged, one critical task remains preparation of the Seder Plate. That is the topic for Chapter 11.

*NINE BRANCH
HANNAKAH
MENORAH*

Reconstruction of the original Temple Menorah as created by the Temple Institute

Summary

Preparation for a successful Passover always includes "cleaning activities" whether part of the public display or not. Indeed, the search for leaven merits discussion and explanation during the official ceremony. The appropriate wear may vary from business attire to casual. Head coverings are optional; however, giving the men and boys a Yakama to wear is always a nice *touch (paper ones are quite inexpensive)*.

The 12-Steps of Passover preparation include 1) Sending the invitations, 2) Shopping, 3) Cleaning, 4) Preparing dinner, 5) Preparing matzah, 6) Preparing wine or grape-juice, 7) Obtaining shank bones, 8) Preparing the charoset, 9) Preparing bitter herbs, 10) washing ceremonial vegetables and dissolving salt, 11) Arranging Seder Plates and finally, 12) Preparing for the arrival of guests.

Table Setting for the left side of the central Seder Table used in a group presentation. Notice the placement of the podium and table items, which can be used for demonstration. During the meal, the table podium is removed, and the young son sits to the right.

CHAPTER 11
THE PASSOVER PLACE SETTING

"Therefore let us celebrate the feast, not with old leaven, nor with the leaven of malice and wickedness, but with the unleavened bread of sincerity and truth."
1 Corinthians 5:8

The Seder Plate

The Seder Plate sits in a prominent place on the Passover table. This central plate is a large one with divisions for each of the symbolic foods. There are some very elaborate plates costing quite a bit of money; however, this is unnecessary. Groups can save money by using a less expensive plate with dividers.

One church, using disposable foil platters for each of its 28 tables, had considerable savings and yet, still produced a pleasant appearance.

The Plate's symbolic foods have remained the same for centuries, except for the boiled egg. Most scholars agree that the egg custom began while the Jews were in Babylonian captivity. Babylon considered the egg as a sign of fertility, and it was often used in their rituals. Some years ago, I decided to substitute the "lowly" mustard seed for the egg. It is Christ's reminder of the importance of faith in our lives—even faith as tiny as the mustard seed. This seemed appropriate because the Passover itself is an extraordinary testament of faith.

The following drawing depicts the layout of the Seder Plate. Note the substitution of the mustard seed for the egg.

The Seder Plate

Seder Plate Ceremonial Foods

1. Christian Passovers can substitute a **mustard seed**, a long-time sign of the Christian faith, for the boiled egg.

2. The roasted **shank bone of a lamb** represents the sacrifice, which was no longer possible after A.D. 70

3. The Seder Plate holds three kinds of bitter herbs: one is a piece of **whole horseradish root,** called *Chazereth* in Hebrew. The other is **freshly ground horseradish**, called *maror*. The third is **parsley,** called *Karpas*. It is the first food eaten at the Seder.

4. Last on the plate is a sweet mixture of **chopped nuts, apples, raisins and cinnamon** called *Charoset*.

OTHER TABLE REQUIREMENTS

The Matzah

In addition to the Seder Plate, there are three more items indispensable to the Passover table: the unleavened bread, the wine or Kosher grape juice, and the Haggadah.

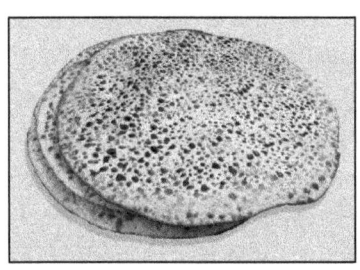

The traditional unleavened bread was flat and irregularly round. It was perforated to prevent excessive bubbling in the dough. When baked, this caused uneven browning, which gave it a striped appearance; hence, it has been called "the bread of affliction." This is meaningful to Christians because of Isaiah 53:5, the description of the Messiah's suffering: *But He was pierced through for our transgressions, He was crushed for our iniquities; The chastening for our well-being fell upon Him, And by His scourging, we are healed.* Thus, eating the bread of affliction becomes a lesson in humility.

There are several explanations behind the matzah symbolism. The first is historical. The Bible tells us that the Israelites left Egypt so quickly that they could not wait for their bread to rise. Matzah then symbolizes the Jews' redemption and freedom. The same is true for Christians because of Jesus' sacrifice on the cross. Biblical references readily call to mind the symbolism for the pierced and striped matzah: *With his stripes we are healed,*[1] and *". . . , so that they will look on Me whom they have pierced; and they will mourn for Him, as one mourns for an only son, and they*

---

[1] Isaiah 53: 5, KJV

will weep bitterly over Him like the bitter weeping over a firstborn...."[2]

Scripture continues, adding an increasing depth and meaning to the matzah that represents Christ's sacrifice: "[6] *All of us like sheep have gone astray, Each of us has turned to his own way; But the LORD has caused the iniquity of us all To fall on Him.* [7] *He was oppressed and He was afflicted, Yet He did not open His mouth; Like a lamb that is led to slaughter, And like a sheep that is silent before its shearers, So He did not open His mouth.*"[3]

The yeast or leaven in the bread is symbolic of corruption and pride. Pride puffs up, as does the yeast. Therefore, yeast is to be avoided during Passover.

Three matzot are placed one on top of the other in a white linen or silk bag or napkin called the *Matzo Tosh*. The bag is square and is usually divided into three compartments, one for each matzah. By Jewish tradition, the three matzot represent a unity. We might agree, seeing one as God, the Father; the broken one as Jesus, the Son; and the third as the Holy Spirit.

The Wine or Kosher Grape Juice

Small wine goblets are placed beside each place setting. They are small because they will be filled four times during the Seder. The custom of drinking four cups of wine dates to ancient temple times. Jewish rabbis have linked the four cups to each of the four verbs used in Exodus 6: 6-7: [6] *"Say, therefore, to the sons of Israel, 'I am the LORD, and I will **bring you out** from under the burdens of the Egyptians, and I **will deliver you** from their bondage. I **will also redeem you** with an outstretched arm and with great judgments.* [7] *Then I **will take you for My people**, and I will be your God; and you shall know that I am the LORD your God, who brought you out from under the burdens of the Egyptians....'"*

One of the wine goblets at the table is usually larger and perhaps more decorated than the others. It is placed at the foot of the table (opposite the leader's position), before an empty chair. It awaits the arrival of Elijah the Prophet, the one who scripture tells us will announce the coming of the Messiah. This is fitting because Passover is identified as the time of redemption. For a large group, this cup may be set only on the table on stage.

Christians may celebrate Elijah's arrival as well, but differently. Jesus stated that John the Baptist was the greatest of all prophets, *"Truly I say to you, among those born of women there has not arisen anyone greater than John the Baptist! Yet the one who is least in the kingdom of heaven is greater than* he.[4]..." Why did Christ say this? It was because other prophets prepared the people for a Messiah who would come. John, however, prepared the people for the Messiah who was imminent. John 1:29 tells us that as Christ approached John for baptism, John singled Him out and said, *"Behold, the Lamb of God who takes away the sin of the world!"*

It is important to remember than John the Baptist also had a unique birth. His mother, Elizabeth, was beyond childbearing years and thought she would die childless. An angel of God appeared to John's father, Zechariah, a Jerusalem temple priest, telling him that his wife would conceive. The angel Gabriel went on to say, *"It is he who will go as a forerunner before Him in the spirit and power of Elijah, to turn the hearts of the fathers back to the children, and the disobedient to the attitude of the righteous, so as to make ready a people prepared for the Lord."[5]* In other words, John was chosen by God to announce the Messiah as the Lord had declared in Malachi 3:1, *"Behold, I am going to send My messenger, and he will clear the way before Me. And the Lord, whom you seek, will suddenly come to His temple; and the messenger of the covenant, in whom you delight, behold, He is coming," says the LORD of hosts."*

The prophet Elijah dressed in a coat of camel's hair as reads 2 Kings 1:8: *"He was a hairy man with a leather girdle bound about his loins." And he said, "It is Elijah the Tishbite."*

John and Elijah were the only prophets to dress this way. Later, Christ explained that Elijah had come before him in the person of John the Baptist: *They asked Him, saying, "Why is it that the scribes say that Elijah must come first?" And He said to them, "Elijah does first come and restore all things. And yet how is it written of the Son of Man that He will suffer many things and be treated with contempt? But I say to you that Elijah has indeed come, and they did to him whatever they wished, just as it is written of him."*[6]

Israel had been without a prophet for more than 500 years,[7] and the crowds turned out in high numbers to hear what this man of God was saying. John's message was straightforward—"Prepare the way of the Lord"—and it was right out of prophecy. Today, Christians recognize that Elijah has already come in the form of John the Baptist. There is no need to prepare for his first coming, only his second. Therefore, we too, place the Cup of Elijah on the Christian Passover table, waiting expectantly for Christ's return.

The Haggadah (The Telling)

The Haggadah is a text that sets forth the order of the Passover Seder, and reading it is a fulfillment of the Scriptural commandment to "tell your son" of the Jewish liberation from slavery in Egypt.

Illuminated German Passover Haggadah – 15th Century.

---

[6] Mark 9:11-13.
[7] Jay Smith, "Book of Malachi Summary," The Bible Hub, 2014.

> **Exodus 13:8**
> *"You shall tell your son on that day, saying, 'It is because of what the LORD did for me when I came out of Egypt.'"*

The exact date of the earliest Haggadah is unknown, but many religious scholars believe that the text of "The Telling" was set down before the time of Christ. The oldest complete manuscript dates back to the 10th century. Initially, all copies of the Haggadah were handwritten.[8] The Jews were quick to adopt printing methods, so the oldest confirmed printed book was in 1482, near Guadalajara, Spain. Even with this, the adopting rate of the printed Haggadah was slow. By the end of the 16th century, only 25 editions had been published, increasing to 37 by the 17th century. [9]

The central portions of the Haggadah text have remained mostly the same since their original compilation. However, over time, changes were made, cumulative songs added, etc. There have been many attempts to modernize the Haggadah in recent times, but the Orthodox Jewish community has resisted this, preferring to adhere to the traditional texts.[10]

A Christian Haggadah
Bay Area Christian Publications

The Christian Haggadah should be scripturally accurate, include history as well as prophetic elements and allow "audience participation."

The *Haggadah Leader's Handbook* is more extensive and contains specific directions for the Seder service. The

---

[8] Jonathan Taub and Yisroel Shaw, *The Malbim Haggadah* (Targum Press, 1990).
[9] Ibid., pp. 23-24.
[10] Ibid., pp. 108-135.

participants will have much smaller, paper-bound editions. The Haggadah tells the participant not only what to do, but when to do it. The *Haggadah Leader's Handbook* describes why it is done. For set-up, the Haggadot may be placed at each place setting on the table.

Summary

The food and table items for this chapter are for a table of six.

Dress for Passover is traditionally more formal than on most days, out of respect for both the Lord and the event; however, modern practices may differ.

The Seder table should be covered with an appropriate but festive tablecloth and accompanying napkins. Each setting should have a plate, flatware, a water glass, a wine (or kosher grape juice) glass, and a Haggadah. Each setting should have a small dish for the salt water.

Light the table with small candles. While not a requirement, the addition of a seven-branch menorah provides an enhanced ambiance.

Near the leader is the *matzo tosh*—a small, square, white silk or linen bag containing three pieces of matzah, one on top of another, separated by napkins.

The wine or kosher grape juice containers are conveniently placed so that the "cups" of the Passover may be poured. Near the end of the table, opposite the leader, is a special goblet for Elijah the Prophet. In a home, there would be only one of these, and the same is true in a large church setting. In both cases, the cup would be set on the leader's table.

The Seder Plate containing the symbolic foods sits before the leader, who will explain their meaning and significance during the service.

In selecting a Christian Haggadah, choose one that provides a clear explanation of the Passover and biblical prophecy of the Christ.

The table is set—the only thing missing is the food for the festive dinner. Chapters 12 and 13 provides advice for its preparation as well as some tested and very delicious Jewish recipes

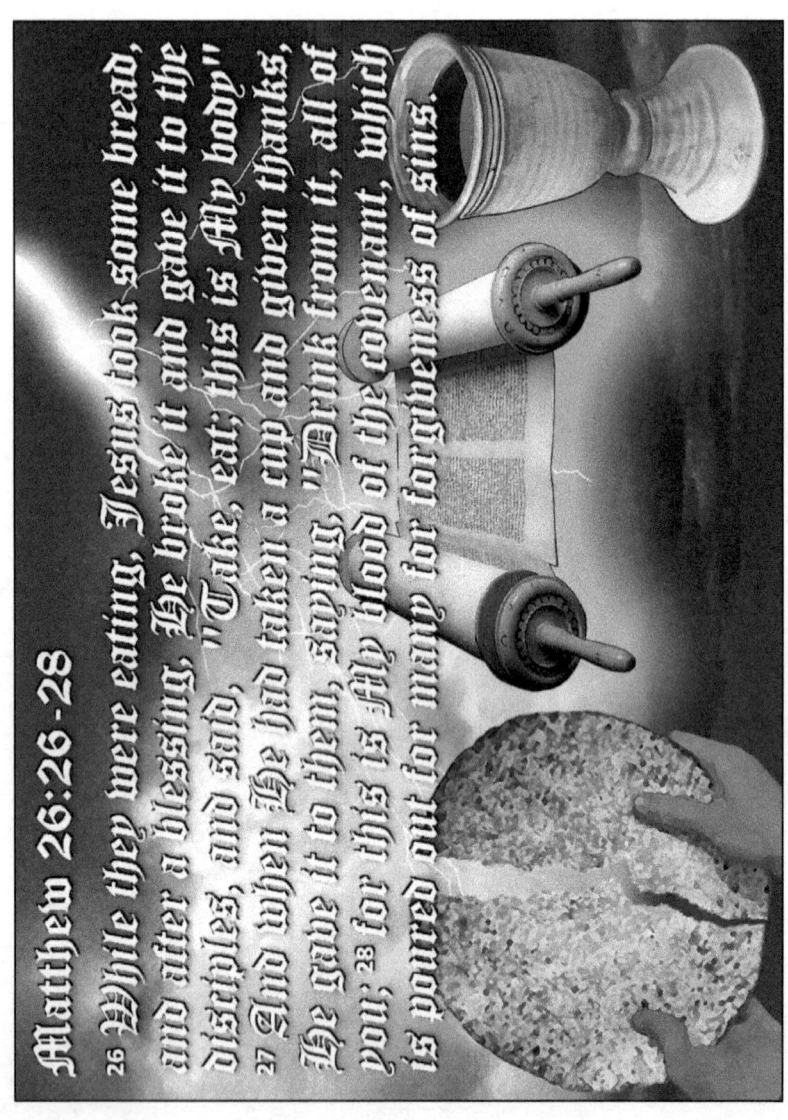

Matthew 26:26-28

26 While they were eating, Jesus took some bread, and after a blessing, He broke it and gave it to the disciples, and said, "Take, eat; this is My body." 27 And when He had taken a cup and given thanks, He gave it to them, saying, "Drink from it, all of you; 28 for this is My blood of the covenant, which is poured out for many for forgiveness of sins.

CHAPTER 12
ANCIENT FOODS OF THE PASSOVER

"So, whether you eat or drink, or whatever you do, do all to the glory of God."
1 Corinthians 10:31

> I am indebted to **Chef Jason Chaney** for his expertise and input into this and the following chapter on food. Chef Chaney, a graduate of the Culinary Institute of New York, was formerly the Chef for the Barbed Rose, one of Houston's top restaurants. Currently, he is the Executive Chef for Houston's Clear Lake City Medical Center. He has extensive expertise in Passover food preparation, and I am grateful to have had his assistance for both Chapters 12 and 13.

Gathering around a table for a meal is a traditional and delightful form of fellowship, not to mention education. The Passover meal was designed to help friends and families, along with large church or organizationally sponsored gatherings, to do both in the spiritual atmosphere of Passover and Holy Week. The meal and its traditional conversations before and during, clearly demonstrate the critical relationships between the Old and New Testament prophecies.

While the temple was in Jerusalem, the focus of the Passover was the sacrificial lamb. Then it was mandatory that every family that was to consume a young lamb offered one for sacrifice at the temple on the 14th day of Nisan [1] and ate it that night, which was the 15th of Nisan.[2] If the family were smaller and couldn't consume the entire offering in one sitting, an offering would be made by a group of families. The

---

[1] Numbers 9:11
[2] Exodus 12:6

offering could not be given with anything that was leavened,[3] and it was required that the lamb is roasted in its entirety, without its head, feet, or inner organs removed.[4] The lamb was to be eaten together with unleavened bread and the bitter herbs. The Hebrews were cautioned not to break any of the lamb's bones from the offering,[5] and none of it could be left over.[6]

Now, in the absence of the Jerusalem temple, the service is celebrated in Jewish homes using symbolic foods, such as the roasted shank bone while the Afikomen substitutes for the lamb. However, many devout Jews have retained the custom of eating lamb during the Seder in memory of the original Seder meal.

The Passover meal is literally a banquet or ceremonial dinner, like the ones at Christmas or Thanksgiving. As Christians, we find even more profound meaning as we celebrate this four thousand years old spiritual tradition.

The Modern Passover Meal:

The modern Passover meal may start with boiled eggs dipped in salt or flavored water. This is followed by appetizers, of which two favorites are chopped liver (like liver pâté) and gefilte fish balls (without sauce and usually made from a "fish paste"—cod or haddock).[7]

---

3 Exodus 23:18
4 Exodus 12:9
5 Exodus 12:46
6 Exodus 12:10; Exodus 23:18
7 Ceil Rosen and Moishe Rosen, *Christ in the Passover* (Chicago: Moody Press, 1978), pp. 50-54.

A matzo ball soup is often served along with dumplings made of matzah and well-beaten eggs. The main course for Jewish families may be a roast fowl or beef. As mentioned earlier, today's Jews usually don't eat lamb because there is no temple, thus no Passover sacrifices. However, some of the more devout Jews may choose to do so.

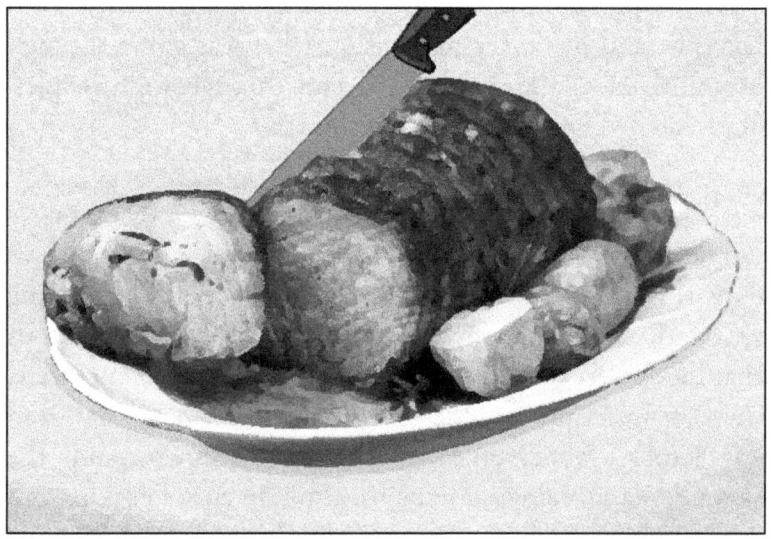

Other foods that accompany the modern Passover meal include salads, vegetables and various desserts including dried fruits, cookies, or coconut macaroons (all made without leaven). Foods that are never set on the Passover table include pork or shellfish. The Torah forbids both.

Our Goal – Preparing an Original Passover Meal

There is little doubt but that we are used to having an abundance of food in today's contemporary diets. Households will have many sweeteners, different types of flour and pastry blends and mixes. In the modern menus of today, we may find any variety of potatoes, tomatoes, and vegetables on the dinner table. However, variation was uncommon during the time of Christ and even less during Moses's era. Therefore, our goal in this chapter is to "get back to the basics" by serving a Passover meal that would contain food items that were available as close to the time of the Exodus as we can get. Although our meal will be unaffected by comparison with present times, it will be rich in symbolic significance.

As you prepare your Passover meal using ingredients from that time and place, try to envision what was going through the minds of the Hebrews then and through the disciples' minds later when they celebrated this feast.

Ancient Jewish Foods

The primary source for knowledge about ancient Jewish foods is the Bible, the most extensive collection of surviving written documents in the world. However, other texts tell us what foods were eaten and what many of the ingredients were. These manuscripts include but are not limited to the Dead Sea Scrolls, Apocryphal works, the Mishnah, and the Talmud.[8] Archaeological remains, also reference items used to produce food, such as wine or olive presses; animal bone remains to provide evidence of meat consumption, the types of animals used, and if they were kept to produce milk or for other uses. Paleo-botanical remains, such as seeds or other plant remains, provide additional information on ancient foods. Using these aids, we can look back at history through written and archaeological data and understand the diet of ancient Israel.[9]

Dietary staples of the Israelites were bread, wine, and olive oil, but they also included fruits, vegetables, and other dairy

---

[8] Oded Borowski, *Daily Life in Biblical Times* (Atlanta, GA: Society of Biblical Literature, 2003).
[9] Ibid.

products or meat, such as fish. Spiritual convictions prohibited the consumption of certain foods such as pork which helped mold the Israelite diet. The meals of ancient Israel were like those of other old Mediterranean areas.[10]

Seven primary agricultural products, called the *Seven Species*, are listed in the Bible: wheat, barley, figs, grapes, olives, pomegranates, and dates.[11] The Bible also describes Israel as a land "flowing with milk and honey."[12] [13]

Barley was the grain most commonly made into flour for bread in Israel.

The Bible, as well as ancient archeology, tells us of some of the cuisine and ingredients that were used during ancient times. Sometimes, the cuisines were used as metaphors in a prophet's vocabulary. Ezekiel did this when he prophesied the fate of Jerusalem by making a stew.[14] The fight between Jacob and Esau was won with a red lentil stew.[15] Then there was the meal Abraham gave the angels before the destruction of Sodom and Gomorrah[16] where we read that young veal was served with milk and butter, along with Sarah's fresh-baked round-bread.

---

[10] Ibid.
[11] Deuteronomy 8:8
[12] Exodus 3:8
[13] Nathan Macdonald, *What Did the Ancient Israelites Eat?* (Wm. B. Eerdmans, 2008). pp. 19–21.
[14] Ezekiel 24: 3-11
[15] Genesis 25: 29-34
[16] Genesis 18: 1-8

The *Book of First Kings* informs us that King Solomon kept finely ground wheat (semolina); fatted beef; game, including venison and fatted geese; and sheep.[17] Back then; vegetables were considered a typical food of the poor (which were most people of the time). This is reinforced in Proverbs, which associates poverty food with a "meal of herbs."[18]

The *Book of Second Samuel* describes a meal where three chieftains meet to honor David and his court. The meal included bread (wheaten and barley) and roasted green wheat, perhaps made into a gruel with roasted brown beans together with freshly roasted lentils. Two different types of meat were served (lamb and beef), along with honey and butter.[19]

The ancient Hebrew daily diet was one of bread, legumes and cooked grains.[20] Bread was served with every meal and vegetables were relegated to a smaller, but significant role. The Hebrews drank goat and sheep's milk when available (spring and summer), and ate cheese and butter. Figs and grapes were common, while dates, pomegranates, and other fruits and nuts were only eaten occasionally. Wine was the most popular beverage, but sometimes other fermented beverages were produced. Olives were grown primarily for their oil. Meat, usually goat and mutton, were rarely eaten and was reserved for special occasions. Game, birds, eggs, and fish were also consumed, depending on their availability.[21] [22]

There were times of famine, and it was then that producing enough food to feed a family required extraordinarily hard work. Irregular climatic conditions also

---

[17] 1 Kings 4: 22-23
[18] Proverbs 15: 17
[19] 2 Samuel 17: 27-29
[20] Claudia Roden, *The Book of Jewish Food* (Penguin Books, 1997), pp. 22–23.
[21] 1 Samuel 25:18
[22] Robert C. Stallman, Dissertation: *Divine Hospitality in the Pentateuch: A Metaphorical Perspective on God as Host* (1999), pp. 159–160.

resulted in unpredictable harvests. Thus, developed the need to save as much food as possible. Consequently, grapes were made into raisins and wine; olives into oil; figs, beans, and lentils were dried; and grains stored for use throughout the year.[23] Most foods were eaten fresh and when in season. Fruits and vegetables were consumed as they ripened.

PRIMARY FOOD INGREDIENTS USED IN ANCIENT ISRAEL

Grains and bread

Typical ancient Israeli hand grinding stone.
Photo by Meule et broyeur du Néolithique

Most foods consumed by ancient Israel were grain products with the staple being bread. At the time, bread was mainly produced from barley flour, but during the Second Temple period, bread from wheat flour was predominant.[24]

---

[23] J. Maxwell Miller and John H. Hayes, *A History of Ancient Israel and Judah*, 2nd ed., (Westminster John Knox Press, 2006), pp. 49–63.
[24] Macdonald (2008), pp. 19–21.

However, the Israelites continued to grow and harvest both wheat and barley. Persia introduced rice to Israel in the during the time of King Herod.

Whole or cracked grain was used to make a gruel or stews, but more frequently, it was ground into flour for the baking of bread which in ancient times, was a daily activity, beginning with the time-consuming task of milling the grain. After the flour was produced, a variety of bread could be made.

Legumes

After grain, legumes (lentils, fava beans, chickpeas, and peas were the main components of the diet and the principal source of protein since meat was rarely eaten.[25] Lentils which were used to make pottages and soups became the most important of the legumes. Cakes baked from ground, roasted lentils were hand pressed and fried in olive oil. David is

---

[25] Ibid., pp. 32–87.

described as providing these cakes to the people as the Ark of the Covenant was brought into Jerusalem.[26]

Lentils and bean stews cooked with onion, leeks, and garlic, were common. The Bible mentions roasted beans and relates how Jacob prepared bread and a pottage of lentils for Esau.[27]

Vegetables

Vegetables are not frequently found in the archaeological records, because plant foods were eaten raw or merely boiled, without requiring special equipment. Consequently, there are hardly any traces, other than the type of food itself.

Wild Lettuce

Commonly eaten vegetables included squash, leeks, garlic, black radishes, and onion. Other herbs such as field greens and root plants were not cultivated but seasonally gathered as they grew in the wild.[28]

Commonly eaten vegetables include squash, onions, leeks, and radishes. Other herbs such as field greens and root plants were not cultivated but seasonally gathered as they grew in the wild.

Wild lettuce was a leafy herb with prickly, red-tinged leaves that became bitter as they matured. These were eaten as a bitter

---

[26] Gil Marks, *Encyclopedia of Jewish Food* (Houghton Mifflin Harcourt, 2010), p. 363.
[27] Genesis 25: 29-34).
[28] Ibid.

herb at the Passover meal. Other bitter herbs included chicory, endive, horehound, reichardia, and wormwood.

Mushrooms, especially of the Boletus type, were harvested in many areas, especially after a significant rainfall. Sesame seeds were also eaten dry and used in the preparation of oil or added to dishes such as stews as a flavoring.

Fruit

Fruit was a vital source of food, mainly grapes, olives, and figs. Grapes were grown for wine, although some were eaten fresh or dried as raisins for storage. Olives were produced for their oil, until sometime after the Roman Empire. Dates, figs, and pomegranates were the other fruits that were eaten.[29]

All the trees, except for the olive, produced fruit that could be eaten fresh or be made into fresh juice. Fruit could also be

---

[29] Macdonald (2008), pp. 28–31.

processed for later consumption in a variety of ways. If it had high sugar content, the fruit would likely be fermented to produce alcoholic beverages; grapes being the most commonly used. Fruit was also boiled down into thick, ultra-sweet syrup. Grapes, figs, dates, and apricots were often dried and preserved individually. Dried fruits, an efficient source of energy, were prepared as provisions for long journeys.[30]

Grapes

Grapes were for production of wine, although they were also eaten fresh and dried to produce raisins, which could then be stored. They were also used to create a thick, honey-like liquid, called grape honey, which was used as a sweetener.

Figs

Figs were an important source of food, especially dried figs. The fruit was cultivated throughout Israel, and fresh or dried figs became part of the daily diet. A common way of preparing  them was to chop the figs and then press them into cakes.[31]

Dates

Dates could be eaten off the tree or even dried, but mostly they were boiled into a thick-rich syrup called "date hone" which was then used as a sweetener. A very "strong drink"

---

[30] Gershon Edelstein and Shimon Gibson, "Ancient Jerusalem's Rural Food Basket," *Biblical Archaeology Review*, Jul–Aug 1982, p. 8
[31] Marks (2010), p. 363.

referenced in the Bible (known as *shechar*) was fermented from the date-syrup.[32] [33]

Pomegranates

Pomegranates were eaten fresh, although occasionally they were used to make juice or wine. They could be sun-dried for use when fresh fruit was out of season. They were symbolically important, as adornments on the hem of the robe of the high priest and the temple pillars.

Other fruits and nuts:

Fruits such as the sycamore fig, mulberry, and possibly the apple were also eaten, but not cultivated. They were picked

---

[32] Marks (2010), p. 363.
[33] Deuteronomy 14: 26

wild when they were in season. Other trees that produced fruits included the carob, which was probably popular due to its sweet taste, and the black mulberry.

Almonds were widespread and eaten along with walnuts and pistachios. The Bible refers to pistachios (*botnim*) and almonds (*shaked*) as "choice fruits of the land" which were sent by Jacob as a gift to Egypt's Pharaoh.[34]

Olives and Olive Oil:

Olives and olive oil were used for food, cooking, and lighting, as well as for sacrificial offerings, ointments, and anointments (King David was anointed).

Olives were ancient Israel's most important natural resource. [35] The tree was well suited to the climate and soil of the Israeli highlands. A substantial portion of the hill country was also allocated to the cultivation of olive trees. Olive oil was more versatile and longer lasting than the oil from other plants, such as sesame, and was considered the best tasting. By the time of the Roman Empire, techniques had been developed to cure olives, first in lye, followed by brine, which would remove olives' natural bitterness, making them edible as food.[36]

---

[34] Genesis 43:11
[35] Macdonald (2008), pp. 28–31.
[36] Borowski (2003).

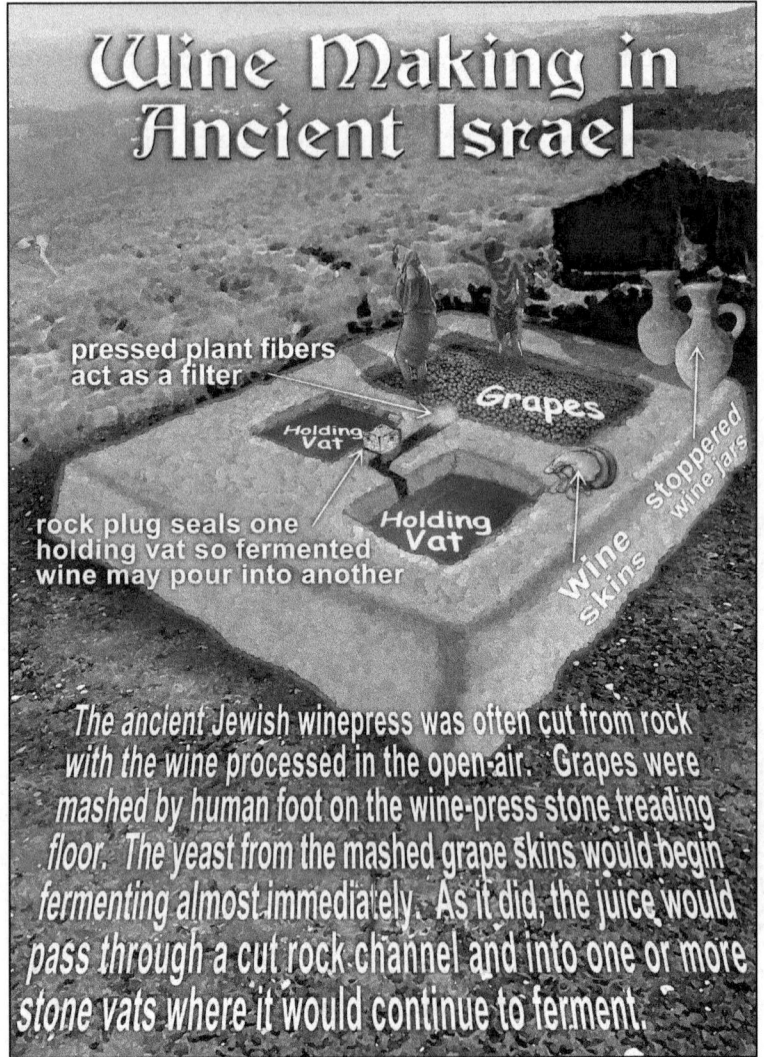

Wine Making in Ancient Israel

pressed plant fibers act as a filter

Grapes

Holding Vat

rock plug seals one holding vat so fermented wine may pour into another

Holding Vat

Wine Skins

stoppered wine jars

The ancient Jewish winepress was often cut from rock with the wine processed in the open-air. Grapes were mashed by human foot on the wine-press stone treading floor. The yeast from the mashed grape skins would begin fermenting almost immediately. As it did, the juice would pass through a cut rock channel and into one or more stone vats where it would continue to ferment.

Wine and other drinks

Israelites usually drank the water that was drawn from wells, cisterns, or rivers. They also drank milk as referenced in Judges 5:25, but often in the form of sour milk, thin yogurt, or whey (usually when available in the spring and summer). They also drank fresh juices from fruits in season as well.

The most preferred strong beverage was wine, although some beer was produced.[37] At the time, the wine was considered an essential part of the diet and a source of calories, sugar, and iron.[38] Most biblical scholars concur that wine was used during the Jewish Seder functions and was also used in many of the other ceremonial services such as weddings and other celebrations. While the wines were stronger than today's store varieties, juices of a less fermented variety were used, particularly for children. Because the wines were often strong, the Bible, while not condemning its conception, frequently warns against intoxicating consumption.

The locally made wines were kept in jars of various sizes and wineskins, both of which are mentioned in New Testament texts. Some faiths treat all mentions of wine in the Bible, as nonalcoholic but this book is not the forum for that debate. However, Bible scholar, Daniel B. Wallace, scores solid points when he writes, *"Some take the words for wine to mean 'grape juice.' If this were so, then why would there be prohibitions against drunkenness? One cannot get drunk on grape juice.*

Further, Jesus' first miracle was changing the water into wine at the wedding of Cana in Galilee. He made between 120 and 180 gallons of wine! Even if this had been grape juice, it would soon turn to wine because the fermentation process would immediately begin. But it most certainly was not grape juice as the head waiter in John 2: 10 says, "Every man sets out the good wine first, then after the guests have drunk freely, the poor wine. But you have kept the good wine until now." [39]

---

[37] Marks (2010), p. 363.
[38] Nogah Hareuveni, *Nature in Our Biblical Heritage* (Israel: Neot Kedumim, 1980).
[39] Ibid., The Biblical Data: Wine and other Alcoholic Beverages in the Bible

It's evident that one may use juice or wine, but if you have a church or organizational Passover, why chance offending anyone. Grape juice will be just fine – but make sure that it is kosher.

For those interested in how the ancient Hebrews made their wine, I refer you to the previous illustration on page 170.

Meat

Israelites ate meat from domesticated goats and sheep. Goat's meat was used the most, as sheep were valued more than goats. Beef and venison were also common foods, and fattened calves provided veal, especially for the wealthy.

Although most meat was obtained from domesticated animals, meat from hunted animals was sometimes available, as the food of Isaac and Esau (Genesis 27:3-4). The remains of gazelle, red deer, and fallow deer are those most frequently discovered in the archaeological record.

Poultry and Eggs

The Israelites consumed domesticated birds, such as pigeons, turtledoves, ducks, along with wild birds (such as quail and partridge). Geese, initially domesticated in ancient Egypt, were also raised in ancient Israel and are most likely the "fattened fowl" that appeared on King Solomon's table.[40]

Chicken became common around the 2nd century B.C., and during the Roman period. Biblical references to eggs refer only to gathering them from the wild.[41] However, eggs increased in use with the introduction of chickens as food.

---

[40] 1 Kings 4: 22-23
[41] Deuteronomy 22: 6-7

Fish

Israelites ate a large variety of fish, both fresh and saltwater. Fishermen supplied the fish to inland communities after they were first dried, smoked, and salted.

Dairy foods

Goats and sheep provided milk for part of the year, and milk and dairy products were a significant source of food. Dairy is mentioned in the Bible, and a frequently repeated description refers to Israel as "a land flowing with milk and honey."[42]

Laban was thick sour milk that was stored in skin containers where it curdled quickly. Another by-product was clarified butter which was used mostly for cooking and frying.

Goat and sheep's milk were the most prevalent types used to produce cheese. Cheese is not often mentioned in the Bible, but in one case, David was sent to take a gift of cheese to the commander of the army.[43]

Honey

The Biblical term *dvash* usually did not mean bee honey, but thick syrup obtained from grapes, figs, or

---

[42] Exodus 3: 8, Exodus 33: 3, Joel 3: 18
[43] 1 Samuel 17: 18

dates. Biblical references to "honey from the crags" (Deuteronomy 32:13), or "honey from the rock" (Psalm 81:16) may refer to fig honey, as fig trees commonly grew in rocky outcrops, or to honey collected from wild bees that made their nests in these places. However, the Bible does occasionally mention honey from bees, as when Samson ate honey from the carcass of a lion[44] or when Jonathan ate honey from a honeycomb. [45] These references referred to honey obtained from the wild.

Seasonings

The most common and yet, essential seasoning was salt,[46] demonstrated by the fact that it is referred to throughout the Bible, and its use was mandated with most sacrifices.[47] Salt was readily available from the Mediterranean or the Dead Sea.

Food was flavored by plants, most native to the region and either cultivated or gathered in the wild, although a few spices were imported. Garlic and onions, and possibly fenugreek, were used to season cooked foods, as well as being eaten as vegetables.

Herbs and spices included capers, coriander, cumin, black cumin, dill, dwarf chicory, hyssop, marjoram, mint, black mustard, reichardia, saffron, and thyme.

Another important seasoning was vinegar, produced by additional fermentation of new wine. It was used for seasoning foods, pickling vegetables, or for medicinal purposes.

---

[44] Judges 14: 8-9
[45] 1 Samuel 14: 25-27
[46] Job 6: 6
[47] Leviticus 2: 13

In Summary

The principal diet of ancient Israel consisted of bread, wine, and olive oil, but also included legumes, fruits, vegetables, dairy products, fish and meat. Except for the wealthy, meat consumption was rare and often limited to the Lord's Feast Days. Olives, figs, and dates were eaten, along with other fruit from the geographical area. Water was the primary drink, followed by wines and goats' milk.

By understanding ancient Israel's fundamental food ingredients, we can develop a far better knowledge of the dishes they would or could have prepared. Though limited in number by today's standards, many old dishes remain that will make your Passover unique for its authenticity. Many of them are discussed in the following Chapter 13.

Durum wheat was the wheat most commonlycultivated in ancient Israel.

CHAPTER 13
THE PASSOVER FEAST

"11 On the day after the Passover, on that very day, they ate some of the produce of the land, unleavened cakes, and parched grain."
Joshua 5:11

The Seder service is the centerpiece of the Passover experience. Overall, an elaborate festive meal takes place on the first or second night of Passover. Family and friends join in celebrating and as we have discussed the Passover Seder, it has some fifteen separate steps that are laid out in the Haggadah (see Chapter 5). This chapter concerns itself with *step ten*, the festive meal (called the Shulchan Orech).

Chapter 12 was devoted to ancient Israeli ingredients for a meal; however, this chapter discusses a traditional Passover menu. It provides recipes for some basic Passover food-dishes that can be served during the feast. There are many more recipes are available, and I would encourage anyone wanting to do so, to research some of the better culinary guides to Jewish cookery including any of the following:

- *Encyclopedia of Jewish Food* (Hardcover) by Gil Marks
- *The Book of Jewish Food* by Claudia Roden
- *The Food of Israel: Authentic Recipes from the Land of Milk and Honey* by Sherry Ansky and Nelli Sheffer

The previous chapter reviewed many food ingredients commonly used in ancient Israel. Many of these are accessible today along with other ingredients and new recipes that are available in modern Jewish cookbooks. There is blank space following each recipe for you to make your food preparation notes as you study the remainder of this chapter.

PREPARING THE SEDER MEAL

It is at the Shulchan Orech that the Narrator if it is a large group or the Table Leader if it is a family setting, announces the meal and "thanks" is given. Although it is Jewish custom to pray following a meal, there were many times when Christ gave thanks before the food, and so we will do this as well.

> **Matthew 14:19**
> *Ordering the people to sit down on the grass, He took the five loaves and the two fish, and looking up toward heaven, He blessed the food, and breaking the loaves, He gave them to the disciples, and the disciples gave them to the crowds.*

Increasing Food Quantities

The following dishes and their recipes are for table settings of six, which is today's average sized dinner table. If your Passover is a group setting of say, twenty tables, then multiply the amount of the food ingredients accordingly.

To begin with, let us learn how to prepare the necessary ritual foods used in the Seder Service, specifically Matzah and Charoset and Maror. This book provides a series of recipes for ancient foods traditionally served at Passover. Other than for the ceremonial foods, please consider the cooking instructions as only a starter for you in your *Passover Journey*. Study the last chapter's list of ingredients that are readily available and adapt them for your church, organization or family's use. Let's start with one of the basics, Matzah.

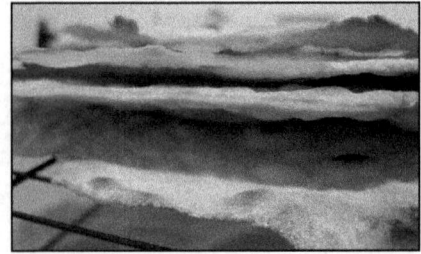

Matzah

The use of matzah in Passover is the oldest symbol of salvation that is in the Seder. Scripture tells us that the Israelites were in such haste to leave Egypt they couldn't wait for their bread dough to rise. Bread, needed for their journey, was the main staple. Leaven was removed from the mix to speed things up and the mixture, when baked, was called matzah. However, matzah also symbolizes redemption and because it is considered a "poor man's bread" it serves as a reminder of humbleness and servitude. Leaven was a symbol of pride because it puffs up as does pride. The Matzah, pierced and stripped as it is, has also become the bread of affliction. The symbolism of matzah is rich indeed.

Matzah is customarily made from flour and water; The flour, formed from either of the five grains mentioned in the Bible (wheat, barley, spelt, rye and oats). Today, matzah is readily available in bakeries and many supermarkets, however, if you want to make it on your own, here is an excellent recipe:

Recipe makes eight matzah pieces of bread

Ingredients:

- 4 - teaspoon all-purpose whole grain flour and extra for rolling
- 3/4 - cup water, or more if needed
- 1 - teaspoon kosher salt, or as needed (optional)
- 2 - teaspoon olive oil, or as needed (optional)

Directions:

Preheat your oven to 475 degrees F. Set a heavy baking sheet on the top rack in the oven to preheat.

Set a timer for 18 minutes, and complete all the steps within that interval. Prepare the work area with 2-teaspoons of flour, or more as needed. Do the same for the rolling pin. Place the flour into a mixing bowl; start the timer; and add the ¾ cups of water, about one tablespoon at a time, into the flour while stirring the water and flour with a fork to form the dough. Remove and place the dough on the prepared work surface, and knead rapidly and firmly until smooth, about a minute.

Divide the dough into four equal segments and then flatten each one and cut in half to get eight segments. Roll each into a ball about 8 inches in size (rolling from the center outward). Use extra flour as needed. The mixture should now be very thin.

Prick holes in the top of the dough (using a fork) to prevent rising. Be sure that the holes go completely through the bread. Afterward, flip each piece over and pierce each, another 25 times with the fork.

Remove the heated baking sheet from the preheated oven, and set the dough lumps onto a baking sheet. Place the baking sheet onto a rack near the top of the stove, and bake for 90 seconds or until golden brown; using tongs turn the pieces over and bake an additional 90 seconds until the bread is light brown and crisp. Keep a watch, not allowing the matzah to get completely brown, or burnt.

Transfer to a wire rack to cool. Lightly brush each matzah with olive oil, and sprinkle with salt.

Notes *(Matzah):*

_____

_____

_____

_____

_____

_____

_____

_____

Charoset

Before the main meal and following the telling of the story of the Exodus, the first real taste of original Jewish food will be a sandwich made from bitter herbs (maror), matzah, and charoset – a sweet  condiment made from ground apples and nuts. The best charoset has the appearance of brown mush because that is what it is. If you prefer a mixture with more smoothness, use a food processor (on pulse mode) rather than stirring. It's difficult to make food that is supposed to resemble mortar look appetizing, but don't worry about the looks, instead focus on the flavor.

Ingredients:

Recipe makes 8 servings

- 1 ½ cups (6 ounces) walnuts, toasted and cooled
- 1 ½ cups (8 ounces) raw almonds, toasted and cooled
- 2 cups tightly packed (3 ounces) dried apples
- 1 1/3 cups (10 ounces) Turkish apricots
- 4 (3-inch long by 1-inch wide) strips orange zest, any white pith removed
- 1 teaspoon allspice
- 1teaspoon cinnamon
- 2 cups ruby Port or medium dry Concord grape wine
- 1 cup golden raisins (3 ounces)

Directions

Stir the apples, walnuts, almonds, and wine together in a large bowl. Season with cinnamon; stir until you have achieved a coarse paste.

Transfer to a bowl and stir in the raisons. Refrigerate until chilled, about 30 minutes.

*Note: Charoset can be made up to 2 days ahead and kept chilled in an airtight container, the flavor does in-fact improve after one day.

Notes *(the Charoset):*

_____

_____

_____

_____

_____

_____

_____

_____

_____

_____

_____

_____

_____

_____

Maror

Bitter Herbs (Maror), is derived from the Hebrew word for "bitter" and consists of horseradish (the whole root or chopped) and lettuce. The lettuce must be wild or Romaine because, after the first bite, it takes on a bitter taste."

Maror refers to the bitter herbs eaten during the Passover Seder and symbolizes the bitterness of slavery in Egypt. A mixture of romaine lettuce and horseradish are the most common vegetables used as bitter herbs. The lettuce isn't bitter at first, but it becomes that way after the first taste, thus making it symbolic of the sin experience. Many modern-day Jewish households use a mixture of cooked horseradish, beetroot, and sugar however traditional Jewish Law forbids flavorings of any kind. You may use the horseradish mixture available in stores but if you want, here is now to make your maror for Passover:

Ingredients: Horseradish roots and Wild or Romaine Lettuce *(which becomes bitter after the first bite)*

Directions:

First, peel the raw horseradish roots and then rinse them thoroughly and dray them carefully, because they will be combined with the matzah later for the Koresh sandwich.

Grate the horseradish with a hand grater or electric grinder.

Use enough horseradish to make a ball the size of an olive and load it on to a leaf of romaine lettuce. This combination is the most common type of maror.

THE PASSOVER FEAST

* Role of bitter herbs in the Seder: the matzah is first eaten, which is followed in turn by maror. Afterward, a maror sandwich (matzah and maror) is combined and consumed.

Notes *(Maror):*

_____

_____

_____

_____

_____

_____

_____

_____

_____

_____

_____

_____

_____

_____

Roasted Leg of Lamb

This recipe produces a very delicious leg of lamb using garlic, lemon, rosemary, thyme, and other seasonings:

Ingredients: (serves 6)

- 1 boned lamb shoulder, rolled & tied about 3 1/2 pounds
- 3 tablespoons olive oil
- 1 finely chopped onion
- ½ cup of chopped leeks
- 3 cloves of garlic, minced
- ½ cup dry white wine
- 1 teaspoon scallions/ 2 tablespoons finely minced parsley
- 1 teaspoon salt
- ½ teaspoon pepper
- ½ cup of chicken stock

Preparation

Season the lamb with salt and pepper. Preheat the oven to 250°.

Brow the lamb on all four sides, by heating the olive oil in a pan. Once browned, remove the lamb and set aside.

Add the onions leeks to the pan and sauté until they are tender.

Place the lamb, fat side up, in a casserole dish. Add the onions and leeks, stock, wine, and scallions. Place in the oven. Bake the lamb for about 5 hours, until extremely tender.

Strain the sauce into a pan, removing as much fat as possible. Place the solids in a food processor, along with 1 tablespoon of the minced parsley. Add this puree to the sauce.

Remove the strings from the lamb. Slice the lamb, then cut it into chunks. Layer the meat into a bowl. Sprinkle the remaining minced parsley over the top, and garnish the platter with parsley. Serve with the sauce on the side.

Notes: *(Roasted Leg of Lamb)*

_____

_____

_____

_____

_____

_____

_____

_____

_____

_____

Matzo Ball Soup

Matzah ball soup is a rich chicken broth with 2 to 4 round Ping-Pong-ball shaped matzah balls. Pieces of carrot or celery are can also be added. This soup is a typical dish served at a present-day Jewish Passover table.

Ingredients (serves 4)

- ½ cup matzah meal
- 2 eggs
- 2 tbsp. oil or schmaltz (melted chicken fat)
- ½ teaspoon salt
- 2 tbsp. water or chicken broth
- 2 tbsp. fresh chopped parsley
- ¼ teaspoon black pepper
- 3 quarts' chicken broth
- 3 carrots cut into chunks
- 2 stalks of celery cut into large pieces

Directions:

Mix the eggs, oil, and water very thoroughly.

Add the matzah meal, black pepper, and parsley and mix. Let the mixture set for thirty minutes so that the matzah meal will absorb the other ingredients.

Bring the chicken broth to a boil and then reduce the heat but keep the broth simmering.

Add the vegetables to the broth.

Wet your hands with water and make 3-5 balls from the mixture. Carefully drop them into the boiling broth. With the heat at a steady simmer, cook the matzah balls for 30-40 minutes.

THE PASSOVER FEAST

Notes: *(Matzo Ball Soup)*

_____

_____

_____

_____

_____

_____

_____

_____

_____

_____

_____

_____

_____

_____

_____

_____

_____

Barley Salad

Here is an excellent salad made with barley and cucumber:

* This side dish is made with barley, which, according to 13th Century traditions, was restricted for use during the Passover. However, I include it here as an example of something eaten in 1st century Passovers. Quinoa is a modern kosher option, which originated in the Americas.

Ingredients (serves 6)

- ½ Cup of Barley
- 2 cups boiling water
- ¼ teaspoon of salt
- ½ Tablespoon extra-virgin olive oil
- 3 Large Cucumbers
- 2 Green Onions (Scallions)

Salad Dressing
- 1 Clove of Garlic, chopped
- 1 Tablespoon Red Wine Vinegar, or Wine Vinegar
- ¼ Cup of chopped basil or mint
- Salt and Pepper to taste
- Arugula for garnish

Directions:

Boil water and stir in the barley and then reduce the heat and simmer for 30 minutes or until it is tender (keeping it partially covered during this time). Drain the barley and set it to the side.

Toss the barley in the olive oil.

Cut, peel and seed the cucumbers into ¼ inch dices. Chop the green onions into ¼ inch lengths.

Blend the dressing ingredients in a small bowl. Next, mix the barley, cucumbers, and green onions with the dressing using a medium bowl.

Once mixed, serve in a bowl garnished with arugula.

Notes: *(Barley Salad)*

_____

_____

_____

_____

_____

_____

_____

_____

_____

_____

_____

_____

_____

Bulgur Gruel

This prepared food, known in Ancient Hebrew as rifot, is one of the most ancient convenience foods referenced twice in the Bible *(Samuel 2, 17:19 and Proverbs 27:22).*

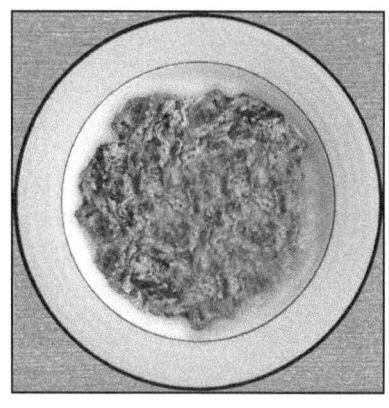

For thousands of years, bulgur was a staple of life. Bulgur is nothing more than wheat berries that have been cleaned, partially cooked, dried and cracked into smaller pieces. The Roman word for bulgur was cerealis; Israelites called it dagan. Other Middle Easterners called it arisah, which is how it is referenced in the Bible.

Bulgur does not need cooking although cooking improves the texture.

Ingredients (Serves: 6):

- 12 oz. coarse-grained bulgur
- 2 oz. olive oil
- 1 small onion, chopped (optional)
- 3 ¼ cups boiling water
- Salt to taste

Directions:

Heat the olive oil in a pan and then carefully fry the onion until it is soft (golden in color). Add the bulgur and fry for 2-3 minutes, until it begins to brown. Stir frequently. Add boiling water, salt and stir well.

Bring to a boil and then reduce the heat and cover. Simmer gently for 15-20 minutes or until all the liquid is absorbed. Then let it set for 10 minutes or so, and then serve.

THE PASSOVER FEAST

Notes: *(Bulgur Gruel)*

_____

_____

_____

_____

_____

_____

_____

_____

_____

_____

_____

_____

_____

_____

_____

_____

_____

Vegetable Sauté

For most of humanity's history, we used and ate the vegetables that were in season. This dish allows you to showcase the best of the season's abundance.

Ingredients (serves 6)

- 2 Tablespoons of wine vinegar 6 globe artichokes, or 1 pound frozen artichoke hearts, thawed
- 2 pounds' fava beans, shelled (about 1 cup), or 1 cup frozen edamame (soybeans), thawed
- 1 pound asparagus cut on a diagonal into 2" pieces
- 3 tablespoons extra-virgin olive oil plus more for drizzling
- 1 medium red onion, finely chopped
- 2 tablespoons thinly sliced fresh mint leaves
- Kosher salt
- Freshly ground black pepper

Directions:

Line a baking sheet with a kitchen towel. Fill a medium bowl with water; add wine vinegar. If using baby artichokes, working one at a time, cut away tough outer leaves until only pale-yellow leaves remain. Cut 1/2" off tops; trim stems. Halve artichokes lengthwise, if desired, then remove choke with a spoon. Place in vinegar water as you finish.

Cook fava beans in a large pot of boiling salted water until just tender, about 2 minutes. Using a slotted spoon, transfer to a bowl of ice water; let cool. Peel and discard outer skins; then convey to a prepared baking sheet. Repeat cooking process with asparagus and artichokes, returning water to a boil between batches and cooling in ice water before moving it to a prepared baking sheet, 3-4 minutes for asparagus and 5-6 minutes for artichokes.

Heat 3 tablespoons oil in a large skillet over medium heat; add onion and sauté until translucent, about 5 minutes. Increase heat to medium-high. Add vegetables and cook, while occasionally stirring, just until heated for about 5 minutes. Season to taste with salt, pepper, and more vinegar, if desired.[1]

Transfer vegetables to a serving bowl. Drizzle with oil; garnish with mint.

Notes: *(Vegetable Sauté)*

_____

_____

_____

_____

_____

_____

_____

_____

_____

_____

_____

---

[1] The Seder Plate - The ingredients and the order of ....
https://www.chabad.org/holidays/passover/pesach_cdo/aid/1998/jewish/The-Seder-Plate.htm

Desert

Since it is highly unlikely that the Passover celebrated in the upper room included a molded ambrosia or pineapple upside down cake, try to keep the dessert options limited. Look back through Chapter 12 at what was available, and serve a variety of seasonally fresh and dried fruit. A platter of fresh cut cantaloupe and watermelon is always a favorite, as are wedges of pomegranate, fresh or dried figs, dried dates (which becomes exotic and divine when soaked overnight in a light honey syrup that has been scented with a bit of rose water), or mix some raisins and walnuts with dried apricots, almonds, and shelled pistachios.

As important as good food is, remember that the Passover is a God ordained time where the focus is not necessarily on the menu, but on recognizing all that the Lord has done to bring ancient Israel and ourselves out of bondage and into the promised land of His incredible grace!

There will be plenty of other opportunities to showcase the molded ambrosia!

Notes:

_____

_____

_____

_____

_____

_____

Tips for Preparing a Successful Passover Meal

1. Prepare as much as you can in advance. There are a lot of small pieces that seemingly come together at once (all at the last minute) in a Passover Seder, so be proactive and knock out what you can in advance and leave as little as possible for the "day of." Inevitably, something always comes up that requires more time than expected; it's better to plan and account for those unexpected moments.

2. Do not overcook the lamb! Lamb is a hard sell as it is today and a person who is reluctant to try it will likely be ruined for life if their first bite is something dry and overcooked. However, flavorful and juicy roasted lamb is delicious and capable of winning over naysayers by the droves. It is also advisable to offer a roasted or smoked fowl (typically chicken) as an alternative for those opposed to lamb.

3. As much as possible, serve the meal family style on each table. There is something about passing food around a table that provides a greater sense of community and fosters more intimate relationships than shuffling in line through a buffet. It may require more food to be made as well as additional bowls and accouterments, but is well worth the trouble.

4. Pray. Have fun and do not forget that you are serving the Lord. With a Christ-centered mindset, all the seemingly impossible work and headache melt away, and nothing remains but the satisfaction of knowing that our Lord is being honored and people are gaining a greater understanding of our God's character and His glorious design and blessings.

"....As for me and my house, we will serve the LORD."
Joshua 24:15

CHAPTER 14
PASSOVER IN THE HOME

" *⁸Let us therefore celebrate the festival, not with the old leaven, the leaven of malice and evil, but with the unleavened bread of sincerity and truth."*
1 Corinthians 5:8

Conducting a Seder in your home for family and friends is the same as doing one for the public, only less cooking and much more comfortable.

THE PASSOVER SEDER IN 3 SEGMENTS
Part 1 occurs before the meal and Part 2, afterwards.

PART ONE (Approximately 50 minutes)

Introduction
Lighting of the Candles
Kiddush – The First Cup
Ur'Chatz – The Washing of Hands
Karpas – Eating of the Green Vegetable
The Symbols of Passover
Yachatz – Breaking the Middle Matzah
The Four Questions
Maggid – Telling the Passover Seder – Responsive Reading
The Second Cup
The Ten Plagues
Dayeinu (Enough)
Motzi – The Bitter Herbs

THE FESTIVE MEAL – *The Shulchan Orech*

PART TWO (Following the meal – Approximately forty minutes)

Bareich – Grace after the meal.
Tzafon – Eating the Afikomen
The Third Cup (The Cup of Redemption)
Waiting for Elijah the Prophet
The Hallel – Psalms of Praise
The Fourth Cup of Praise (The Cup of Taking Out)
Nirtzah – Conclusion of the Seder

Preparing for the Home Seder

It is customary, but not a requirement, that spring-cleaning accompany the family search for leaven. Leaven is, after all, to be removed from the house for Passover and only unleavened foods served. This can be a financial chore should you have a collection of bread, chips, flours, and other items with leaven. If you want to be traditional and remove all leaven, but you are concerned about the cost, find a friend who is not conducting Passover and get her to take possession of your leaven products. According to Jewish law, she should buy them from you. A Jewish rabbi provided the method: sell the items for $1.00. Afterward, you repurchase them for the same price.

After you determine the number of people attending, begin to prepare the room and the table. Because the Passover for the Christian is symbolic of Christ's sacrifice, you may want to place a picture or painting of Jesus in the room. You may want to add other festive decorations, because this is a celebration of our salvation from sin, just as it was for the Hebrews' deliverance from slavery.

The table items for a home Passover are the same as those for a public one. However, the effort for a home-based celebration for a family of six or eight people is significantly less than for a much larger Passover program.

The following chart provides a list of what is needed:

Requirements for a Home Passover (*Family of 8*)

1. **Two *Leader's Handbooks:*** one for each the two leaders, perhaps the husband and wife.

2. **Haggadot**, one for each person in attendance. The husband and wife will not need one, because they will read from the *Leader's Handbooks.*

3. **A "nice" linen tablecloth**: Others may be used, but white linen tends to cost less and always seems appropriate as the Christian nears the Easter season.

4. **Plate and tableware settings for eight**: This is the time to use your best. It may be simple or elaborate. The key is that it is your best for the Lord.

5. **Kosher grape juice or kosher wine:**[1] Wine was originally used, but a kosher grape juice is fine. The only difference between the

---

[1] Kosher grape juice or kosher wine: Kosher wine or grape juice is either drink produced according to Judaism's religious law, specifically, the Jewish dietary requirements. The United States of America contains roughly 40% of the Jewish population of the world, and most US wine stores, particularly in the northeast, have a small kosher section. Today, there are thousands of kosher wines that are available in every conceivable style from virtually all the world's wine-producing regions.

two is 12%.[2] If using a kosher wine, a dry, less sweet one is recommended.[3]

6. **Beverage glasses:** One for wine or juice, the other is for water *(two glasses per person).*

7. **Cup of Elijah**: a separate container for the prophet is placed at the end of the table, opposite the leader.

8. **The ritual foods**: *maror, bitter herbs*, and *matzah* are placed on the table – Recipes are in Chapter 12.

9. **One Seder Plate** is placed near the leader *(See Chapter 11).*

10. **One seven-lamped menorah** is available to be lit during the candle-lighting ceremony.

11. **Small bowls for salt water** are on the table; one for each person in attendance.

12. **Yamaka caps:** are optional but nice touches for the men and boys and it adds to the room's ambiance.

Role Playing for the Seder

The biblical commandments concerning the Passover stress the importance of continuing to remember events and God's commandments.[4] [5] We know that we learn by doing. God knew that before we did, which is why I am sure that He instituted the Passover memorial as a service. Aside from passing on prophetical biblical wisdom to family members, it can be a great testimony and outreach to those who do not know Christ. At every opportunity, open the ceremony up to participation and role-playing. Questions, answers, and discussion will further this goal. The latter would be too unwieldy for a public Seder but is perfect for an intimate home

---

[2] There are low alcohol wines (3% - 7%) available. There are many brands to be found in stores, markets or the Internet.
[3] Kosher wine - Wikipedia. https://en.wikipedia.org/wiki/Kosher_wine
[4] Deuteronomy 16: 12
[5] Exodus 13: 3

setting. The latter would be too unwieldy for a public Seder but is perfect for an intimate home setting. That is why it is crucial that the two lead roles (the Priestly Figure and the Narrator) study their *Leader's Handbooks* beforehand. It is reasonably self-explanatory and contains much useful material aside from the Haggadah.

The Seder Roles:

The Seder Leader (referred to in the Haggadah as the Priestly Figure): Biblically, the head of the house must always take this role. If there is no husband, a woman may assume the position. However, if a grandfather lives in the home, he may also take on the role. The Seder leader sits at the head of the table.

The Narrator: The wife or senior woman in attendance assumes this role. If a grandmother lives in the household, she may also take the role. The narrator should sit in a position where she works best with the Priestly Figure.

The Young Boy: The youngest boy traditionally asks the "Four Questions" posed in the Haggadah and sits to the right of the Priestly Figure. The apostle John is thought to have been the youngest and would have sat to the right of Christ. John would have been the one who asked the questions.

Other Roles: Other roles include the child who seeks the Afikomen or the one who opens the door for Elijah and later closes it. Involvement helps the entire family. A daughter may help the mother in the candle-lighting ceremony just as a son may assist in the hand washing or pouring of the cups. An attending friend may offer the "before dinner" grace. A child could read Christ's Parable of the Mustard Seed. It is short and appears in three of the New Testament Gospels. The differences between Matthew 13:31–32, Mark 4:30–32 and Luke 13:18–19 are minor. Matthew and Luke include it immediately followed by the Parable of the Leaven, which carries the theme of the Kingdom of Heaven growing from small beginnings. Having both read, one after the other is very appropriate.

There are sections in the Christian Haggadah calling for responsive reading, which is yet another way to engage those attending your Seder. Remember, the more involvement you have of family and friends, the more they will learn from the service.

The Use of Music

Jewish music adds quality to any Seder. As explained in earlier chapters, the background music is widely used for a public Seder. It is spaced, timed, and thematic to the moment, very much like a film score. This isn't necessary for the home Seder because the music is there as background, to add a dimension to the service and pleasure during the meal.

Instrumental music is useful as a background because it does not interfere with the teaching, talking, or listening. Keep the music at the right level by turning it down until you cannot hear it; then turn up the volume until you can barely hear it. You will now have the perfect background music for your Passover.

READY TO GO?

The home is ready, the table is dressed, and the food is prepared. Guests have arrived and taken their seats. The following is a step-by-step guide that will carry you through each of the three segments of the Passover Seder discussed earlier in this chapter.

This will be easy if you merely follow the instructions in the *Leader's Handbook*, remembering that the in-home Seder is smaller and less formal. The *Handbook* calls for songs, but you may or may not do this, as you wish.

＿ ＿ ＿ ＿ ＿ ＿ ＿ ＿ ＿ ＿ ＿ ＿ ＿

The In-Home Passover – Step by Step

Step 1: The Seder leader (the Priestly Figure) welcomes everyone and makes a simple introduction, telling those attending what he or she may expect and why the home Passover is being done. Do not make this so formal—keep it warm and personable. In the Home Passover, the honored wife serves as the Narrator. She reads from the Leader's Handbook. The guests can easily follow along by reading from and using the personal Haggadot that is on the table.

> **Note**: the *Leader's Handbook*, while written for large groups, may easily be used for the in-home Seder. It contains detailed instructions in addition to supplying "Director Notes" sections where you can enter notations pertaining only to the more personal up-close ceremony. The in-home leader takes the role of the Priestly Figure, and the wife or senior woman, the role of narrator.

Step 2: Candle-Lighting Ceremony—After the narration is read, the honored wife leads in the candle-lighting ceremony.

Step 3: The first cup is poured, and the *Leader's Handbook* is read. The Seder leader officially carries out the duties of the Passover service, but it is the narrator who explains to others what is happening and why. Following the explanations, the first cup is consumed.

Step 4: The leader explains the biblical basis for the "Washing of Hands" ceremony. The narrator further explains and instructs the guests in the washing. They will use a pitcher and water bowl that may be on the table or a nearby sideboard. If you have two bowls, the service will go much more quickly.

Step 5: At this time the leader explains the eating of the green vegetable, and the narrator instructs them when to do so.

Step 6: The biblical "Breaking of the Bread" or middle matzah is carried out by the leader. This section of the Passover has a direct prophetic connection to Christ. It is interesting because it was written before His birth. The leader removes the middle matzah from the covering called the "matzo tosh" and breaks it. The narrator explains the significance. One of the broken pieces, the Afikomen, is hidden. Have the children cover their eyes while an adult hides it in the room. If there are no children present, the narrator may symbolically hide the Afikomen for later discovery.

Step 7: The leader provides an explanation of "the three symbols" that represent the original three symbols of Passover at the time of Moses. One by one, he briefly discusses the lamb, the matzah and the bitter herbs. The tie-in to the Christian should, of course, be made.

Step 8: The leader announces that this is the time for eating the matzah and bitter herbs. The narrator instructs the guests to join in by using the materials that are supplied on the table. Everyone takes a piece of matzah and when cued, dip it in bitter herbs (the horseradish) and eat.

Step 9: The leader explains to the guests how to eat the matzah and bitter herb sandwich. The sandwich is made up of the matzah, bitter herbs, and the mortar or apple and nut mix. The narrator goes further and explains the "sop" referenced in New Testament Scripture. The "sop" is the matzah sandwich dipped in the bitter herbs. It is given to a loved one at the table. Jesus dipped his sop and handed it to Judas, who then left to betray Him. Those unfamiliar with Passover will have missed this act of love by Christ during His last supper.

Step 10: Grace before the meal is given; someone may offer it other than the leader or narrator.

Step 11: Part One ends and Part Two of the service begins. The time for eating the Passover meal has arrived. This section is called the Shulchan Orech, meaning festive meal. The wife or narrator should explain the authenticity of the foods—many dating back thousands of years. The person cooking the food might discuss the ingredients. Many people are surprised to learn that the honey referred to in the Bible was usually not bee's honey. Explain that although the modern-day Passover is without lamb, a lamb was traditional before Christ and for some 30 years after His death and resurrection. Explain, therefore, that lamb will be eaten at the evening's Passover meal.

This is an excellent place to ask whether anyone has questions. The time may also be used for instructional purposes. Don't let the discussion become lengthy because people will be hungry and want to eat. After the meal ends, the third section of the Seder will begin.

Step 12: The third section of the service starts with the *Four Questions*. The narrator explains why the youngest at the table sits at the leader's right *(the youngest who can ask the questions)*. The leader and child go through all the questions, explaining each as they are being asked.

Step 13: The Passover story is told with help from guests who will read responsively, as led by the narrator.

Step 14: The second cup of wine is poured, lifted in a toast, but not drunk. The narrator has the guests replace their cups, and the leader carries them through an explanation of the Ten Plagues. As the plagues are named one by one, each guest removes one drop of liquid from his or her cup, placing it on a plate or napkin.

Step 15: *Dayeinu* is Hebrew, meaning "enough for us." Traditionally at this point, God is praised for what He has done for us, recognizing that at any point in His blessings, had He stopped, it would have been enough for us. At the conclusion, the Dayeinu Song is usually sung. It is an easy one to learn, and it can be found on any number of Internet websites. In fact, all the words and music are on **Wikipedia** at their *Dayeinu* entry. **YouTube** also carries the music live under **Dayeinu** or **Passover Song** (Judaica).

Step 16: Instructions are given for drinking the second cup of wine.

Step 17: The leader gives the Bareich or "grace" after the meal.

Step 18: Eating the Afikomen is a significant time in the meal, for it was here that Jesus took the bread, broke it, and gave it to His disciples. Christians celebrate this moment today as Communion. The children are instructed to search for the Afikomen. The one who finds it is given a token reward by the honored wife. Afterwards, the narrator explains the significance of the moment and the leader leads everyone in Communion.

Step 19: The third cup, the Cup of Redemption, is the cup that Christ passed to his disciples as he instituted the second part of the Communion service. The guests are instructed to drink the cup.

Step 20: The final and last cup (the fourth cup) is also called the Cup of Redemption. On the table sits a separate container called the Cup of Elijah. In the Jewish tradition, this Cup of Redemption is poured, but not drunk. It remains on the table as a sign of God's messianic promise of renewal. However, we understand as Christ explained, *"11They asked Him, saying, "Why is it that the scribes say that Elijah must come first?" 12And He said to them, "Elijah does first come and restore all things. And yet how is it written of the Son of Man that He will suffer many things and be treated with contempt? 13 But I say to you that Elijah has indeed come, and they did to him whatever they wished, just as it is written of him."* [6]

Step 21: The fourth cup remains as hymns of praise are sung. These are called the Hallel. Usually, the songs are taken from

[6] Mark 9: 12-16

Psalm 113 to 118 (considered the Passover Psalms). A suitable Christian song may also be sung.

Step 22: All now drink the fourth cup of wine, which has two other names, the Cup of Praise and Completion or the Cup of Taking Out. At this point, Matthew quotes Jesus as saying, *"But I say to you, I will not drink of this fruit of the vine from now on until that day when I drink it new with you in My Father's kingdom."* [7] This moment may be followed by another hymn of praise.

Step 23: This step represents the conclusion of the Seder. A thank-you for attending is appropriate, as is a final prayer. The costs of the Haggadot, no matter which ones you decide upon, are small. You may permit your guests to take them in remembrance. Who knows? You may be successful in having them continue the tradition in their homes. At the very least, you will have been effective in providing valuable moments of Christian instruction. As with many things we are called upon to do, we are sowers of seeds. It is up to the Lord to grow them.

— — — — — — — — — — — — —

As you will discover, the combination of the *Passover Leader's Handbook* and accompanying *Haggadah* provide excellent guidance through the entire ceremony. At the end of your Seder, attendees are frequently enthusiastic and excited and may have further questions. This is an excellent time to talk more about the meaning of Passover and to answer their queries on a less formal basis. The Seder ends, the guests have left and the family has retired to bed. The Christian Passover service is over. The first thing to do afterwards is to thank the

---

[7] Matthew 26: 29

Lord for the honor of providing such an event and pray Him to use it for his glory. Naturally, you will want to thank Him for the help he gave you.

Immediately after the ceremony or as early the following day as possible, it's a good thing to take notes on the previous evening's event. Jot down those things that you want to do differently or perhaps emphasize more of, next year. If there were errors, make a note of that as well.

As you pack items away, treat them like your Christmas ornaments. Place them where than can be easily found for your next years' service.

Also, consider sending a "thank you" note to each guest (outside of your family) who attended.

In Summary

The in-home Passover is very much like the ones that are publicly offered, only much more straightforward. Naturally, there is still food to prepare, but for fewer people. There is the preparation of the Seder table, but only one. As with the public service, there should be a rehearsal for those with speaking roles.

Success in anything lies in planning, organizing, rehearsing, and execution. The better you do the first three, the more successful the last one will be. If you have further questions, return to the relevant chapters in this book. Remember: do not hesitate to seek help from your Jewish friends.

Above all, thank God for the help He has given you and the opportunity to serve Him.

APPENDICES

APPENDIX A: THE PASSOVER SCRIPT
APPENDIX B: PASSOVER CHECKLISTS

APPENDIX A – The Passover Script

APPENDIX A.
THE PASSOVER SCRIPT

THE FOLLOWING SCRIPT, TO BE PERFORMED BY ACTORS IN A STAGE SET BEFORE AN AUDIENCE, INVOLVES A HIGH DEGREE OF COLLABORATIVE EFFORT. TIME EXPENDED IN PRACTICE IS VERY WORTHWHILE. THE BETTER THE SCRIPT IS PERFORMED, THE MORE REWARDING IT WILL BE FOR YOUR PASSOVER ATTENDEES.

A QUICK READING OF THE SCRIPT WILL DEMONSTRATE THAT YOUR SEDER ACTORS HAVE A HIGH INTERACTION WITH THE PASSOVER LEADER OR NARRATOR. EVERYONE INTERACTS WITH MUSIC, SOUND EFFECTS, LIGHTING, AND SOUND. IN OTHER WORDS, ALTHOUGH THE SCRIPT IS RELIGIOUS IN NATURE, IT NO LESS PARALLELS A SCENARIO FOR A THEATRICAL PRODUCTION. INDEED, EVEN FOR SMALL CHURCHES, THIS IS A MAJOR PRODUCTION. THE DIFFERENCE BETWEEN A SMALL AND A LARGE PASSOVER IS MERELY THE SIZE OF ITS PRODUCTION.

ALTHOUGH THE FOLLOWING SCRIPT IS COMPLETE, ITS SIZE (NECESSARY FOR THIS BOOK) IS TOO SMALL FOR COMFORTABLE READING OR REFERENCE. ASIDE FROM THE PROBLEMS OF COPYRIGHT VIOLATIONS, IT IS BETTER TO ORDER ACTUAL SCRIPT COPIES FOR THE CAST AND CREW MEMBERS.

THE PASSOVER SCRIPT

PASSOVER ORDER OF SERVICE AND BANQUET SCRIPT[1]

45 MINUTES OF RECORDED PRELUDE MUSIC: *PLAY 45 MINUTES BEFORE THE SERVICE BEGINS. THE RECORDING MAY BE SHORTENED TO ALLOW FOR—*

LIVE OPENING MUSIC

---

[1] Prepared from the oldest manuscripts available at the time of printing and the exceptional work of David Sargent in his *Messianic Passover Haggadah*, God and Science Organization, July 13, 1992, used with permission. Also, insights from, *Seven Feasts of Israel*, by Zola Levitt, Zola Levitt Ministries, 1979.

FOLLOWING THE PRELUDE MUSIC, THE PASSOVER SEDER BEGINS.

WELCOME AND INTRODUCTION

BACKGROUND MUSIC FADES AS MINISTER/ELDER WALKS TO DOWNSTAGE AREA

OPENING WELCOME AND INTRODUCTION PROVIDED BY THE MINISTER OR SENIOR ELDER. BACKGROUND MUSIC ENDS AS WELCOME ENDS.

SPOTLIGHT ON SHOFAR BLOWER

[SPOTLIGHT PICKS UP THE BLOWER OF THE SHOFAR (THE RAM'S HORN) AS HE WALKS DOWNSTAGE LEFT TOWARD AUDIENCE – HE RAISES THE SHOFAR TO ITS PLAYING POSITION....]

A SOUND OF THE SHOFAR – THIS IS BEST PERFORMED LIVE, BUT IF NOT, A PRERECORDED SHOFAR BLAST MAY BE SUBSTITUTED. WHETHER LIVE OR RECORDED, IT IS VERY EFFECTIVE TO HAVE A COSTUMED FIGURE REMINISCENT OF AN EARLY HEBREW PERIOD TO "BLOW" THE SHOFAR.

[SHOFAR PLAYER EXITS TO FAR STAGE RIGHT AND WAITS.]

FADE ALL LIGHTS TO BLACK

OFFSTAGE VOICE OF GOD: (PRE-RECORDED VOCAL ADDING APPROPRIATE REVERB SOUNDS)

I AM GOD, AND THERE IS NO OTHER; I AM GOD, AND THERE IS NONE LIKE ME. I MAKE KNOWN THE END FROM THE BEGINNING, FROM ANCIENT TIMES, WHAT IS STILL TO COME. THESE ARE MY APPOINTED FEASTS, THE APPOINTED FEASTS OF THE LORD, WHICH YOU ARE TO PROCLAIM AS SACRED ASSEMBLIES.

*THESE ARE THE **LORD'S** APPOINTED FEASTS, THE SACRED ASSEMBLIES YOU ARE TO PROCLAIM AT THEIR APPOINTED TIMES: THE **LORD'S** PASSOVER BEGINS AT TWILIGHT ON THE FOURTEENTH DAY OF THE FIRST MONTH; ON THE FIFTEENTH DAY OF THAT MONTH, THE **LORD'S** FEAST OF UNLEAVENED BREAD BEGINS.*

BACKGROUND MUSIC UP

SPOTLIGHT ON NARRATOR WITH DIM LIGHT ON TABLE

NARRATOR: TONIGHT, WE CELEBRATE THE PASSOVER FEAST THAT JESUS ATTENDED THE EVENING BEFORE HIS CRUCIFIXION. THIS IS OFTEN REFERRED TO AS "THE LAST SUPPER."

IN THE CENTER OF YOUR SEDER TABLE IS THE SEDER PLATE. IT IS A SPECIAL PLATE WITH EACH FOOD ON IT HAVING A SYMBOLIC MEANING. EACH SYMBOL – THE MATZAH, THE ROASTED LAMB BONE, THE BITTER HERBS, THE GREEN VEGETABLE, THE CHAROSES OR CLAY, AND THE SALT WATER – WILL BE EXPLAINED DURING THE SERVICE. HOWEVER, ONLY THE LAMB, THE MATZAH AND BITTER HERBS ARE COMMANDED BY THE TORAH FOR PASSOVER. THE OTHER FOODS HAVE LONG BEEN PART OF THE PASSOVER SERVICE FOR CENTURIES. ON THE OTHER HAND, WE HAVE EXCLUDED THE "ROASTED EGG," WHICH SCHOLARS BELIEVE WAS ADDED DURING THE BABYLONIAN CAPTIVITY. IN THE BACK OF YOUR HAGGADAH IS AN EXPLANATION FOR EACH OF THESE ITEMS.

THE QUESTION HAS BEEN RAISED AS TO WHY WE, AS BELIEVERS IN JESUS, TONIGHT CELEBRATE IS A JEWISH HOLIDAY – PASSOVER. THERE ARE SEVERAL REASONS:

♦ WHEN GOD INSTITUTED HIS FEASTS, THE HEBREW WORDS HE USED INDICATED THAT THESE FEASTS WERE BOTH

"APPOINTED TIMES" AND SACRED "ASSEMBLIES." TODAY, WE WOULD CALL THESE FEASTS "REHEARSALS."

* PASSOVER WAS AN IMPORTANT EVENT IN THE HISTORY OF THE NATION OF ISRAEL. DURING THAT TIME, GOD PROVIDED AN ESCAPE FROM DEATH FOR THE FIRSTBORN SON OF EACH HOUSEHOLD. HE DID THIS BY ACCEPTING AS A SUBSTITUTE FOR THE DEATH OF THE FIRSTBORN, THE BLOOD OF A LAMB.

* IT WAS DURING A PASSOVER THAT GOD FORESHADOWED THE ESCAPE FROM DEATH FOR ALL MANKIND: THE ACCEPTANCE OF THE BLOOD OF HIS FIRSTBORN SON, JESUS, AS A SUBSTITUTE FOR THE PRICE OF OUR SINS.

* THUS, THE PASSOVER WAS ALSO A REHEARSAL OF ANOTHER EVENT IN THE HISTORY OF MANKIND: THE PERFECT SACRIFICE ON THE CROSS, THE FULFILLMENT OF WHICH IS JESUS CHRIST.

* WE KNOW FROM HISTORY THAT THOUSANDS OF JEWS WERE SO CONVINCED THAT JESUS WAS BOTH LORD AND MESSIAH THAT THEY, WHO WERE JEWS, BECAME THE FIRST "CHRISTIANS." THEY UNDERSTOOD THAT JESUS FULFILLED THE MESSIANIC PROPHECIES OF SCRIPTURE.

* THE JEWISH PASSOVER OF TODAY STILL POINTS TO YASHUA, WHICH IS THE HEBREW NAME FOR JESUS.

* GOD SPECIFICALLY CHOSE THE JEWISH NATION AS THE CUSTODIAN OF THESE ORACLES OF GOD. AS CHRISTIANS, WE SHOULD BE ETERNALLY GRATEFUL.

BACKGROUND MUSIC FADES

THE ORDER OF SERVICE

SPOTLIGHT ON NARRATOR

NARRATOR: THE MEAL TONIGHT WILL BE CELEBRATED TRADITIONALLY AS IT HAS BEEN SINCE THE FIRST PASSOVER, THOUSANDS OF YEARS AGO. APART FROM THE

PLACEMENT OF THE MEAL, THE ORDER OF SERVICE, CALLED THE "SEDER," COMES FROM THE MOST ANCIENT OF AVAILABLE REFERENCE *HAGGADOT*. RABBIS OF THE TIME PRESCRIBED THE CONTENT OF THE HAGGADAH TO MAKE SURE THAT THEY FULFILLED THE COMMAND IN EXODUS THAT "YOU SHALL TELL YOUR SON OF THE EXODUS."

TONIGHT, WE WILL FOLLOW AN ANCIENT HAGGADAH. ADDED TO IT ARE NOTES AND COMMENTARY TAKEN FROM BOTH EARLY AND LATE JEWISH AND CHRISTIAN RESOURCES. THERE IS A TRANSLATED COPY FOR YOU ON YOUR TABLE. WE ENCOURAGE YOU TO USE IT TO FOLLOW ALONG IN THE SERVICE AND TAKE IT HOME FOR FUTURE REFERENCE.

"WINE" BACKGROUND MUSIC UP

A WARNING ABOUT WINE

FOUR CUPS OF WINE WILL BE POURED AND DRUNK BY EACH PARTICIPANT TONIGHT. TRADITIONALLY THE FOUR CUPS USE EITHER A KOSHER WINE OR A KOSHER GRAPE JUICE. WHETHER ONE USES KOSHER WINE OR GRAPE JUICE, EACH IS DERIVED FROM THE "FRUIT OF THE VINE," GRAPES. REMEMBER THAT THE DIFFERENCE BETWEEN THE TWO IS THE GRAPE JUICE IS NOT FERMENTED, WHEREAS THE WINE IS APPROXIMATELY 12% ALCOHOL BY VOLUME. THEREFORE, BECAUSE WE WANT THE CHILDREN TO EXPERIENCE THE PASSOVER SEDER, WE HAVE CHOSEN TO USE THE "KOSHER GRAPE JUICE" AS OUR FRUIT OF THE VINE.

"WINE" BACKGROUND MUSIC FADES

EACH CUP IS TO BE TOTALLY DRUNK TO SYMBOLIZE THE COMPLETENESS OF OUR JOY. WITH THAT IN MIND, YOU MAY ELECT NOT TO COMPLETELY FILL YOUR CUP AS YOU ARE SERVED.

SPOTLIGHT ON PRIESTLY FIGURE

SEARCHING FOR LEAVEN

PRIESTLY FIGURE: *WE BEGIN OUR PASSOVER BY "SEARCHING FOR LEAVEN."*

SPOTLIGHT ON NARRATOR

"WINE" BACKGROUND MUSIC UP

NARRATOR: IN A JEWISH HOME, PASSOVER IS A TIME OF PREPARATION AND CELEBRATION. THE MOTHER COOKS SPECIAL FOODS, BRINGS OUT PLATES AND UTENSILS AND CLEARS THE HOUSE OF ALL LEAVENING MATERIALS.

IN SCRIPTURE, "LEAVEN" REPRESENTS A SYMBOL OF SIN, KNOWN BY RABBIS AS "THE EVIL INCLINATION." BEFORE MODERN YEAST CONTROL, ALL BREAD WAS OF A SOURDOUGH TYPE. AN OLD LUMP OF DOUGH, CONTAINING THE YEAST OR LEAVEN, WAS ADDED TO THE NEW DOUGH TO MAKE IT RISE. LIKEWISE, SIN IS PASSED FROM ONE GENERATION TO THE NEXT, WHICH IS BIBLICAL. PEOPLE OFTEN SAY, "HEY, LISTEN, I AM ONLY MORTAL." WHAT IS MEAN IS THAT SIN IS AT THE HEART OF OUR BEING.

THE NIGHT BEFORE THE FIRST DAY OF PASSOVER, AT THE BEGINNING OF THE FEAST OF UNLEAVENED BREAD, THE HEAD OF THE HOUSES MAKES FINAL PREPARATION FOR THE PASSOVER BY FIRST SEARCHING FOR LEAVEN THROUGHOUT THE HOME. THIS PUTTING AWAY OF LEAVEN IS A PICTURE OF SANCTIFICATION.

"WINE" BACKGROUND MUSIC FADES

SPOTLIGHT ON PRIESTLY FIGURE

PRIESTLY FIGURE: *BLESSED ART THOU, O LORD OUR GOD, RULER OF THE UNIVERSE, WHO MADE US SACRED WITH HIS COMMANDMENTS, AND DIRECTED US TO DO AWAY WITH THE LEAVEN.*

227

SPOTLIGHT ON NARRATOR

NARRATOR (AS BOY SEARCHES): AT THIS POINT, THE YOUNG USUALLY SEARCH FOR LEAVEN BREAD TO SEE IF ANY REMAINS IN THE HOUSE. CUSTOMARILY, A FEW CRUMBS ARE LEFT FOR THE CHILDREN TO FIND. ONCE THE LEAVEN IS DISCOVERED (ALL OF IT), IT IS TOSSED INTO A FIREPLACE, OR WRAPPED AND DISCARDED.

> [YOUNG BOY AT TABLE BEGINS SEARCHING FOR PIECES OF LEAVEN. AS HE FINDS THEM, HE PLACES THEM IN A SMALL WHITE LINEN BAG.]

> [REAL OR PRERECORDED SOUNDS OF CHILDREN LAUGHING ARE HEARD.]

SPOTLIGHT ON PRIESTLY FIGURE

PRIESTLY FIGURE: THE APOSTLE PAUL WROTE OF LEAVEN AND PASSOVER IN 1ST CORINTHIANS 5: 6-7: ^{6}... "DO YOU NOT KNOW THAT A LITTLE LEAVEN LEAVENS THE WHOLE LUMP OF DOUGH? ^{7}CLEAN OUT THE OLD LEAVEN SO THAT YOU MAY BE A NEW LUMP, JUST AS YOU ARE IN FACT UNLEAVENED. FOR CHRIST, OUR PASSOVER ALSO HAS BEEN SACRIFICED." THEREFORE, LET US KEEP THE FESTIVAL, NOT WITH THE OLD LEAVEN, THE LEAVEN OF MALICE AND WICKEDNESS, BUT WITH BREAD WITHOUT LEAVEN, THE BREAD OF SINCERITY AND TRUTH."

COLLECTED LEAVEN (THE CHAMET) IS OFTEN BURNED AS PART OF THE CEREMONY.

THE LIGHTING OF THE CANDLES
THE WOMEN'S BLESSING

PRIESTLY FIGURE: IT IS NOW TIME FOR THE LIGHTING OF THE FESTIVAL LIGHTS.

SPOTLIGHT ON NARRATOR AND

LIGHT THE FAMILY AT TABLE

NARRATOR: PER HEBREW TRADITION, ISRAEL WAS REDEEMED FROM EGYPT BECAUSE THE WOMEN OF THAT GENERATION WERE MORE RIGHTEOUS THAN THE MEN. TO BEGIN OUR SEDER, WE WILL FOLLOW TRADITION BY GRANTING THE SENIOR WOMAN OF THE HOUSEHOLD THE HONOR OF LIGHTING THE FESTIVAL LIGHTS.

WILL THE HONORED WOMAN AT EACH TABLE, THE MOST SENIOR, PLEASE LIGHT THE CANDLES ON THEIR TABLE?

[WHEN FINISHED, THE HONORED WIFE SINGS THE FOLLOWING BLESSING.]

HONORED WIFE (OR RECORDING): *BARUCH ATAH ADONAI, EL-O-HAY-NU MEL-ECH HA-O-LAM, SHE-SHA-LACH ET BIN-'E-CHA Y-'E-CHID-'E-CHA, YASHUA HA-MA-SHI-ACH, LIH-'E-YOT OR HA-O-LAM, V-'E-SEH HAP-PES-ACH, SHE-LAN-U L-'E-MA-AN NICH-'E-YEH BIZ-'E-CHUTO. AMEN*

ALL WOMEN TOGETHER: *BLESSED ART THOU, O LORD OUR GOD, KING OF THE UNIVERSE, WHO HAS SENT THY SON, THINE ONLY SON, YASHUA THE MESSIAH, TO BE THE LIGHT OF THE WORLD AND OUR PASSOVER LAMB, THAT THROUGH HIM WE MIGHT LIVE. AMEN.*

SPOTLIGHT ON PRIESTLY FIGURE

PRIESTLY FIGURE: Y'VAREKH-EKAH ADONAI V'YISHMAREKHA, Y'AER ADONAI PANAVELEKHA V'HUNEKHA, Y'ISAH ADONAI PANAVELEKHA, V'ASEMLEKHA SHALOM]

THE LORD BLESS YOU AND KEEP YOU; THE LORD MAKE HIS FACE SHINE UPON YOU AND BE GRACIOUS TO YOU; THE LORD LIFT UP HIS COUNTENANCE UPON YOU AND GIVE YOU PEACE.

KIDDUSH: *THE FIRST CUP*

SPOTLIGHT ON NARRATOR

NARRATOR: Everyone, please fill your First Cup.

SPOTLIGHT ON PRIESTLY FIGURE

[The PRIESTLY FIGURE fills his First Cup as all attending fill their First Cups.]

PRIESTLY FIGURE: Let the Seder begin.

[Lifts the Kiddush and says...]

PRIESTLY FIGURE: This first cup is the "Cup of Sanctification and Blessing." IN HEBREW, it is called the KIDDUSH. With this cup, we set this night aside as different from all other nights.

Ba rook Ah-tah Ah-doh-nai El-o-hay-nu Mel-ick Ha-oh-lam Boray P'ree Ha gah-fen. Amen.

LIGHT FOR PERFORMERS

SPECIAL MUSIC – THE VINEYARD SONG

FADE PERFORMER LIGHT FOR SPOTLIGHT ON PRIESTLY FIGURE

PRIESTLY FIGURE: Blessed art Thou, O Lord our God, Ruler of the universe, Creator of the fruit of the vine. Amen.

Blessed art Thou, O Lord our God, Ruler of the universe, who sent Your only Son that we might have life and have it more abundantly. May we remain holy by placing our faith in Him and by following His commandments.

Blessed art thou, O Lord our God, Ruler of the universe, who has given us life and brought us to this happy season.

230

SPOTLIGHT ON NARRATOR

NARRATOR: BEFORE FLEEING EGYPT, THE HEBREWS DID NOT HAVE THE PRIVILEGE OF RECLINING DURING MEALS AS THEIR CAPTORS DID. HOWEVER, ONCE FREED, THEY COULD DO SO AND DID SO DURING PASSOVER BY RECLINING TO THE LEFT ON A PILLOW. WHEN PILLOWS WERE UNAVAILABLE, THEY CONTINUED TO CELEBRATE THIS PRIVILEGE BY DRINKING FROM THE CUP WHILE LEANING SLIGHTLY TO THE LEFT. TONIGHT, WE WILL DO THE SAME. WILL YOU PLEASE LEAN SOMEWHAT TO THE LEFT AND DRINK THE CUP.

[ALL LEAN TO THE LEFT AND DRINK THE CUP.]

UR'CHATZ (THE WASHING OF HANDS)

SPOTLIGHT ON PRIESTLY FIGURE

PRIESTLY FIGURE: *NOW FOR THE UR'CHATZ OR THE WASHING OF HANDS:*

BACKGROUND MUSIC UP

PRIESTLY FIGURE: *FROM EXODUS, WE LEARN THAT "HE PLACED THE LAVER BETWEEN THE TENT OF MEETING AND THE ALTAR AND PUT WATER IN IT FOR WASHING. FROM IT, MOSES AND AARON AND HIS SONS WASHED THEIR HANDS AND FEET. WHEN THEY ENTERED THE TENT OF MEETING, AND WHEN THEY APPROACHED THE ALTAR, THEY WASHED, JUST AS THE LORD HAD COMMANDED MOSES."*

PRIESTLY FIGURE: *BLESSED ART THOU, O LORD OUR GOD, KING OF THE UNIVERSE, WHO HAS SANCTIFIED US WITH THY COMMANDMENTS AND COMMANDED US TO WASH THE HANDS.*

SPOTLIGHT ON NARRATOR

231

NARRATOR: EVERYONE ATTENDING TONIGHT SHOULD PLEASE WASH YOUR HANDS USING THE PITCHER AND LARGE BOWL ON YOUR TABLE; AFTERWARD YOU MAY DRY THEM WITH THE PROVIDED TOWEL. PLEASE START ON THE LEFT AND WORK AROUND THE TABLE.

SPOTLIGHT ON PRIESTLY FIGURE

PRIESTLY FIGURE: *AT THE TIME OF THE FIRST CUP, DURING JESUS' LAST PASSOVER SUPPER, THE BIBLE TELLS US THAT – DURING THE WASHING OF HANDS – CHRIST DID SOMETHING ELSE:*

"[3]JESUS, KNOWING THAT THE FATHER HAD GIVEN ALL THINGS INTO HIS HANDS AND THAT HE HAD COME FORTH FROM GOD AND WAS GOING BACK TO GOD, [4]*GOT UP FROM SUPPER, AND *LAID ASIDE HIS GARMENTS; AND TAKING A TOWEL, HE GIRDED HIMSELF. [5]THEN HE *POURED WATER INTO THE BASIN AND BEGAN TO WASH THE DISCIPLES' FEET AND TO WIPE THEM WITH THE TOWEL WITH WHICH HE WAS GIRDED. [6]SO HE *CAME TO SIMON PETER. HE *SAID TO HIM, "LORD, DO YOU WASH MY FEET?" [7]JESUS ANSWERED AND SAID TO HIM, "WHAT I DO YOU DO NOT REALIZE NOW, BUT YOU WILL UNDERSTAND HEREAFTER." [8]PETER *SAID TO HIM, "NEVER SHALL YOU WASH MY FEET!" JESUS ANSWERED HIM, "IF I DO NOT WASH YOU, YOU HAVE NO PART WITH ME.' [9]SIMON PETER SAID TO HIM, 'LORD, THEN WASH NOT ONLY MY FEET BUT ALSO MY HANDS AND MY HEAD.' [10]JESUS SAID TO HIM, 'HE WHO HAS BATHED NEEDS ONLY TO WASH HIS FEET, BUT IS COMPLETELY CLEAN; AND YOU ARE CLEAN, BUT NOT ALL OF YOU.' [11]FOR HE KNEW THE ONE WHO WAS BETRAYING HIM; FOR THIS REASON HE SAID, "NOT ALL OF YOU ARE CLEAN."

[12]" SO WHEN HE HAD WASHED THEIR FEET, AND TAKEN HIS GARMENTS AND RECLINED AT THE TABLE AGAIN, HE SAID TO THEM, "DO YOU KNOW WHAT I HAVE DONE TO YOU?"

JOHN 13: 3-12

BACKGROUND MUSIC FADES

KARPAS *(EATING OF THE GREEN VEGETABLE)*

SPOTLIGHT ON PRIESTLY FIGURE

PRIESTLY FIGURE: *THIS A TIME FOR THE* **KARPAS,** *WHICH IS "THE EATING OF THE GREEN VEGETABLE."*

GREEN IS A SYMBOL OF LIFE AND SPRINGTIME, AND THE SALT WATER IS TO REMIND US OF THE TEARS SHED BY THE OPPRESSED HOUSE OF ISRAEL IN EGYPT.

BA ROOK AH-TAH AH-DOH-NAI EL-O-HAY-NU MEL-ICK HA-OH-LAM BORAY P'REE HAH-AH-DAH-MAH.

BLESSED ART THOU, O LORD OUR GOD, RULER OF THE UNIVERSE, CREATOR OF THE FRUIT OF THE EARTH.

SPOTLIGHT ON NARRATOR

NARRATOR: EVERYONE SHOULD NOW EAT YOUR GREEN VEGETABLE, WHICH IS THE PARSLEY THAT YOU WILL DIP IN THE SALT WATER.

> [ALL EAT THE GREEN VEGETABLE, PARSLEY DIPPED IN SALT WATER.]

YACHATZ *(BREAKING THE MIDDLE MATZAH)*

SPOTLIGHT ON PRIESTLY FIGURE

PRIESTLY FIGURE: *NOW IS THE* **YACHATZ** *OR "THE BREAKING OF THE MIDDLE MATZAH.*

BACKGROUND MUSIC UP

[PRIESTLY FIGURE DISPLAYS THREE MATZAHS WRAPPED IN WHITE COVERING OR NAPKIN.]

PRIESTLY FIGURE: THE RABBIS HAVE RIGID CODES AS TO THE APPEARANCE OF THE MATZAH. IT MUST HAVE STRIPES, BE PIERCED AND BE WITHOUT LEAVEN. THE PROPHET ISAIAH, INSPIRED BY GOD, SPOKE OF THE MESSIAH YET TO COME. THESE VERSES PROVIDE A PERFECT DESCRIPTION OF YASHUA WRITTEN HUNDREDS OF YEARS BEFORE HIS BIRTH – FOR IT WAS JESUS WHO WAS TAKEN OUT AND AFFLICTED, STRIPED, PIERCED AND WAS WITHOUT SIN.

SPOTLIGHT ON NARRATOR

NARRATOR: FOR BELIEVERS IN YASHUA, WE COME NOW TO ONE OF THE MOST FASCINATING PARTS OF THE SEDER, THE BREAKING OF THE MIDDLE MATZAH. THREE MATZAHS ARE PLACED IN A SPECIAL WHITE COVERING CALLED THE "MATZO TOSH." *(MATZO TOSH)*

LIGHT PRIESTLY FIGURE AS HE DEMONSTRATES – LIGHT REMAINS ON NARRATOR

[PRIESTLY FIGURE DEMONSTRATES AS THE NARRATOR DISCUSSES.]

NARRATOR: THE MIDDLE MATZAH IS REMOVED AND BROKEN. THE LARGER PIECE IS WRAPPED AND HIDDEN. THIS PIECE IS CALLED THE *AFIKOMEN,* WHICH MEANS, "THAT WHICH COMES LATER," OR LITERALLY TRANSLATED FROM THE GREEK, "I CAME." THE AFIKOMEN IS HIDDEN, OR BURIED, TO BE FOUND AND LATER REDEEMED FOR A REWARD.

THIS PART OF THE CEREMONY HAS PUZZLED RABBIS THROUGHOUT THE CENTURIES. FIRST, WHY ARE THERE THREE MATZAHS? TO SOME RABBIS, THE THREE MATZAHS REPRESENT THE **HIGH PRIEST, LEVITES,** AND **PEOPLE** OF **ISRAEL** – THE THREE FORMS OF WORSHIP IN TEMPLE TIMES. BUT WHY IS THE MIDDLE PIECE BROKEN? THAT REMAINS UNEXPLAINED.

ANOTHER GROUP OF RABBIS CLAIMS THAT THE THREE MATZAHS REPRESENT **ABRAHAM, ISAAC,** AND **JACOB.** BUT THIS CLAIM TOO DOES NOT EXPLAIN WHY THE MIDDLE MATZAH IS BROKEN.

STILL, OTHER RABBIS CLAIM THAT IN THE WILDERNESS, GOD GAVE DAILY **MANNA,** WITH A DOUBLE PORTION GIVEN ON FRIDAY, AND ONE MORE IS ADDED FOR PASSOVER, MAKING THREE. BUT WHY IS THE MIDDLE MATZAH BROKEN, BURIED AND BROUGHT BACK? THIS SPECIFIC PASSOVER TRADITION HAS BEEN CELEBRATED FOR THOUSANDS OF YEARS WITHOUT EXPLANATION.

HOWEVER, FOR BELIEVERS IN CHRIST, IT IS NO MYSTERY. THIS PART OF THE CEREMONY BECOMES A BEAUTIFUL PICTURE OF THE ONE GOD, REVEALED IN THE FATHER, SON, AND HOLY SPIRIT.

[PRIESTLY FIGURE ILLUSTRATES AS THE NARRATOR EXPLAINS.]

NARRATOR: THE WHITE LINEN BAG REPRESENTS THE TRINITY. THE SON, JESUS CHRIST, LEFT THE HOLY OF HOLIES REPRESENTED BY THE BAG. HE WAS BROKEN, BURIED, AND BROUGHT BACK - ALL PER OVER 300 OLD TESTAMENT PROPHECIES, WHICH WERE LITERALLY FULFILLED APPROXIMATELY 2,000 YEARS AGO.

BUT WHY DOES THE ONE WHO FINDS THE "BURIED" PIECE OF MATZAH RECEIVE A REWARD? TO THE BELIEVER IN CHRIST, THIS TOO IS OBVIOUS. THE PERSON WHO FINDS AND ACCEPTS THE LORD RECEIVES THE REWARD OF SALVATION AND ETERNAL LIFE.

LIGHT OFF NARRATOR

[PRIESTLY FIGURE UNCOVERS THE MATZAH AND LIFTS THE PLATE [OR SMALLER MIDDLE

MATZAH] FOR ALL TO SEE, THEN RECITES THE FOLLOWING–]

PRIESTLY FIGURE: THIS IS THE BREAD OF AFFLICTION, WHICH THE ISRAELITES ATE IN THE LAND OF EGYPT. TO THE CHRISTIAN, IT REPRESENTS THE BODY OF OUR LORD JESUS.

SPOTLIGHT ON NARRATOR - OFF PRIESTLY FIGURE

NARRATOR: TRADITIONALLY, AT THIS POINT IN THE SERVICE, THE JEWS OVER THE CENTURIES HAVE ASKED THAT THEIR SERVITUDE END. THEY FURTHER REQUEST THAT NEXT YEAR AT PASSOVER, THEY MAY BE IN THE LAND OF ISRAEL. KNOWING OF THE SECOND COMING OF OUR LORD JESUS CHRIST, WE MAKE A SIMILAR REQUEST.

BACKGROUND MUSIC FADES

SPOTLIGHT ON PRIESTLY FIGURE

PRIESTLY FIGURE: NOW, WE ARE SLAVES OF THE FLESH AND OPPRESSED BY THE WORLD; NEXT YEAR, MAY WE BE FREE MEN AND WOMEN. TODAY, WE ARE HERE; NEXT YEAR, MAY WE BE WITH OUR LORD AND SAVIOR WHEREVER HE MAY BE. IN THIS WAY, WE EAGERLY LOOK FORWARD TO THE RETURN OF CHRIST.

[BREAK THE MATZAH. THE PLATE IS SET ASIDE, AND THE MATZAH IS COVERED.]

SPOTLIGHT ON NARRATOR

NARRATOR: PLEASE POUR A CUP OF WINE IN PREPARATION FOR THE SECOND CUP, WHICH WILL COME LATER.

[POUR THE CUP, BUT DO NOT DRINK IT.]

SPOTLIGHT ON PRIESTLY FIGURE

PRIESTLY FIGURE: Now we will **HIDE** the **AFIKOMEN.** All the children's eyes are to be closed.

SONG FOR HIDING OF AFIKOMEN

SPOTLIGHT ON FAMILY

[As the song is sung, the Honored Wife proceeds to the back of the room, where she hides the Afikomen. The Priestly Figure returns the other matzah to its cover.]

THE THREE SYMBOLS

SPOTLIGHT ON PRIESTLY FIGURE

PRIESTLY FIGURE: Now, we proceed with the explanation of "The Three Symbols."

BACKGROUND MUSIC UP

The rabbis say, "Whoever does not repeatedly explain the following three symbols at the Seder on Passover has not fulfilled his duty." Those symbols are –

* **THE PASSOVER OFFERING, WHICH IS THE LAMB**
* **THE MATZAH**
* **THE BITTER HERBS**

PRIESTLY FIGURE: The Passover offering, which the Israelites ate in temple days, is explained because the Holy One, blessed be He, passed over the houses of their forefathers in Egypt. As written in Exodus 12:26-27: "26 And when your children say to you, 'What does this rite mean to you?' 27 you shall say, 'It is a Passover sacrifice to the Lord [a]who

PASSED OVER THE HOUSES OF THE SONS OF ISRAEL IN EGYPT WHEN HE SMOTE THE EGYPTIANS, BUT [AD]SPARED OUR HOMES.'" AND THE PEOPLE BOWED LOW AND WORSHIPED."

AS CHRISTIANS EAT LAMB ON PASSOVER, THEY ARE REMINDED THAT GOD PROVIDED US WITH HIS SON AS THE "PASSOVER LAMB" FOR OUR SALVATION.

[PRIEST RAISES A MATZAH TO ABOVE EYE LEVEL.]

PRIESTLY FIGURE: THE SECOND SYMBOL, THE MATZAH, WHICH WE EAT, REMINDS THE CHILDREN OF ISRAEL THAT THERE WAS NOT ENOUGH TIME FOR THE DOUGH OF THE ISRAELITES IN EGYPT TO LEAVEN, OR RISE BEFORE THEY WOULD BE CALLED OUT OF EGYPT. AS IT IS TOLD IN THE BOOK OF EXODUS, "34 SO THE PEOPLE TOOK THEIR DOUGH BEFORE IT WAS LEAVENED, WITH THEIR KNEADING BOWLS BOUND UP IN THE CLOTHES ON THEIR SHOULDERS. 39 THEY BAKED THE DOUGH WHICH THEY HAD BROUGHT OUT OF EGYPT INTO CAKES OF UNLEAVENED BREAD. FOR IT HAD NOT BECOME LEAVENED SINCE THEY WERE DRIVEN OUT OF EGYPT AND COULD NOT DELAY, NOR HAD THEY PREPARED ANY PROVISIONS FOR THEMSELVES." - (EXODUS 12: 34,39)

LIKEWISE, TODAY WE ARE TO PREPARE OUR HEARTS AND SOULS WITHOUT LEAVEN SO THAT WE WILL BE READY TO LEAVE IMMEDIATELY UPON CHRIST'S SECOND COMING.

[PRIEST HOLDS UP THE BITTER HERBS.]

PRIESTLY FIGURE: THESE ARE THE BITTER HERBS, WHICH WE EAT. WHAT IS THEIR MEANING? THEY ARE EATEN TO RECALL THAT THE EGYPTIANS EMBITTERED THE LIVES OF THE ISRAELITES, AS IS WRITTEN IN EXODUS, "AND THEY EMBITTERED THEIR LIVES WITH HARD LABOR; WITH MORTAR AND BRICKS, WITH EVERY KIND OF WORK IN THE FIELDS; ALL THE WORK WHICH THEY MADE THEM DO WAS RIGOROUS."

SO TOO THE CHRISTIAN WILL RECALL SACRIFICES MADE THROUGH THE CENTURIES BY THOSE WHO DIED FOR THE CAUSE AND FAITH IN JESUS CHRIST, OUR MESSIAH.

BACKGROUND MUSIC FADES

MATZI (MATZAH, MAROR, AND KORECH)

SPOTLIGHT ON PRIESTLY FIGURE

PRIESTLY FIGURE: NOW IS THE TIME FOR THE MATZAH, WHICH IS MADE UP OF THE MATZAH, MAROR, AND KORECH.

SPOTLIGHT ON NARRATOR

NARRATOR: AT EACH TABLE, PLEASE LOCATE AND PASS OUT THE MIDDLE AND TOP MATZAH THAT YOU WILL FIND THERE.

[ATTENDEES PASS OUT THE MIDDLE AND TOP MATZAH. THE PRIESTLY FIGURE HOLDS UP THE MIDDLE MATZAH.]

PRIESTLY FIGURE: BAROOK ATAH AH-DOH-NAI ELOHAY-NU MELICK HA-OH-LAM HA-MOH-TZI L'HKEM MEEN HA AH-RETZ. AMAIN. BLESSED ART THOU, O LORD OUR GOD, RULER OF THE UNIVERSE, WHO BRINGS FORTH BREAD FROM THE EARTH.

[THE PRIESTLY FIGURE HOLDS UP THE TOP MATZAH]

PRIESTLY FIGURE: BLESSED ART THOU, O LORD OUR GOD, RULER OF THE UNIVERSE, WHO MADE US HOLY WITH HIS COMMANDMENTS, AND COMMANDED US CONCERNING THE EATING OF MATZAH.

SPOTLIGHT ON NARRATOR

NARRATOR: Everyone should now eat the matzah.

[*Everyone eats the matzah.*]

MAROR - *Bitter Herbs*

BACKGROUND MUSIC UP

SPOTLIGHT ON PRIESTLY FIGURE

PRIESTLY FIGURE: *Now for the Maror and the Bitter Herbs.*

Blessed art Thou, O Lord our God, Ruler of the universe, who made us holy with His commandments, and commanded us concerning the eating of bitter herbs. (Exodus 12:8 & Numbers 9:11) Eat the bitter herbs.

SPOTLIGHT ON NARRATOR

NARRATOR: Now everyone should eat the matzah dipped in bitter herbs.

[*Everyone eats the matzah.*]

KORECH -- MATZAH, BITTER HERBS SANDWICH

SPOTLIGHT ON PRIESTLY FIGURE

PRIESTLY FIGURE: *Now is the Korech – which is the eating of the Bitter Herbs and Matzah Sandwich.*

PRIESTLY FIGURE: *In remembrance of the holy temple, we do as the rabbis did in temple times. The rabbis put matzah and bitter herbs together and ate them as a sandwich, to observe the words of*

THE TORAH LITERALLY; "THEY SHALL EAT IT [THE PASSOVER OFFERING] WITH MATZAH AND BITTER HERBS."

SPOTLIGHT ON NARRATOR

NARRATOR: EVERYONE SHOULD NOW PREPARE A SANDWICH. IT WILL BE MADE OF THE MATZAH, BITTER HERBS, AND MORTAR, OR THE APPLE MIX. AFTERWARD, YOU WILL EAT THE SANDWICH.

[ATTENDEES MAKE A SANDWICH OF MATZAH, BITTER HERBS AND MORTAR (THE APPLE MIX)].

NARRATOR: BEFORE YOU EAT THE SANDWICH, THIS SANDWICH WAS EATEN WITH LAMB DURING TEMPLE TIMES IN JERUSALEM. IT IS ALSO KNOWN AS THE "SOP." AS IN THE PAST, IT IS STILL THE CUSTOM TODAY TO GIVE A SOP DIPPED IN THE BITTER HERBS TO A LOVED ONE. YOU SHOULD NOW GIVE YOUR SOP TO A LOVED ONE AT YOUR TABLE.

[ONCE THE SOPS ARE PASSED TO THE LOVED ONES, THE ATTENDEES ARE TO EAT THE SANDWICHES.]

SPOTLIGHT ON PRIESTLY FIGURE

[PRIESTLY FIGURE HANDS THE DIPPED SOP TO HONORED WIFE, WHO IN TURN GIVES IT TO THE YOUNG BOY.]

BACKGROUND MUSIC FADES

PRIESTLY FIGURE: IT WAS WITH THE DIPPED SOP THAT YASHUA SPOKE OF HIS BETRAYAL IN THE NEW TESTAMENT IN JOHN 13: 21-28: [21] WHEN JESUS HAD SAID THIS, HE BECAME TROUBLED IN SPIRIT, AND TESTIFIED AND SAID, "TRULY, TRULY, I SAY TO YOU, THAT ONE OF YOU WILL BETRAY ME." PETER MOTIONED JOHN TO ASK WHO THE BETRAYER WAS. "[26] JESUS THEN ANSWERED, 'THAT IS THE ONE FOR WHOM I SHALL DIP THE MORSEL AND GIVE IT TO

HIM." [30] SO AFTER RECEIVING THE MORSEL HE WENT OUT IMMEDIATELY..." AND WE KNOW, THAT JUDAS THEN BETRAYED THE MESSIAH.

LIGHT FOR PERFORMERS

SPECIAL MUSIC - "WHY"

SPOTLIGHT ON NARRATOR

NARRATOR: JEWISH CUSTOM IS TO HAVE GRACE AFTER A MEAL, AND WE WILL FOLLOW THIS CUSTOM. HOWEVER, JESUS GAVE THANKS MANY TIMES BEFORE HE ATE, AS WE READ IN MATTHEW, "AND LOOKING UP TOWARD HEAVEN, HE BLESSED THE FOOD."

SPOTLIGHT ON PRIESTLY FIGURE

PRIESTLY FIGURE: LET US NOW GIVE THANKS.

[PERSONAL PRAYER OF THANKS, PERHAPS GIVEN BY THE MINISTER OR SENIOR ELDER OF THE CHURCH]

SHULCHAN ORECH (THE FESTIVAL MEAL)

PRIESTLY FIGURE: NOW IT IS TIME FOR THE SHULCHAN ORECH, WHICH IS "THE FESTIVAL MEAL."

LET THE MEAL BEGIN!

SPOTLIGHT ON NARRATOR

NARRATOR: ALL FOODS SERVED TONIGHT ARE AUTHENTIC JEWISH PASSOVER FOOD. MANY ARE MADE FROM RECIPES STRETCHING BACK CENTURIES, WITH SOME PREPARED THOUSANDS OF YEARS AGO. PLEASE HELP YOURSELF. AS WE DISCUSSED EARLIER, TRADITIONALLY NO ROASTED LAMB WAS SERVED FOR THE ORTHODOX PASSOVERS AFTER THE LOSS OF THE JEWISH TEMPLE IN A.D. 70.

HOWEVER, TONIGHT WE DO HAVE LAMB BECAUSE JESUS HAS FREED US FROM THE TRADITIONAL TEMPLE SACRIFICE.

LIGHT OF CENTER STAGE SPEAKERS

[NARRATOR EXPLAINS HOW THE SERVING WILL BE DONE DEPENDING UPON THE FACILITY, TABLE PLACEMENT, ETC. AT THIS POINT IN THE SERVICE, THERE IS A TYPICAL "LULL" AS PEOPLE ARE BEING SERVED OR HELPING THEMSELVES. TO ADD INTEREST AS WELL AS TO EDUCATE, THE NARRATOR AND PRIESTLY FIGURE MAY CONDUCT A MINI-EDUCATION BLOCK DISCUSSING MATERIAL PERHAPS NOT KNOWN BY THE GENERAL ATTENDEES. IT IS ALSO AN EXCELLENT PLACE FOR A BRIEF QUESTION AND ANSWER PERIOD. ALL OF THIS WILL TAKE UP DOWNTIME AND QUICKEN THE PACE OF THE SERVICE, BEING CAREFUL THAT THIS COVERS ONLY THE SERVING TIME, NOT THE MEALTIME.]

***

[AS THE MEAL ENDS—THE SHOFAR IS BLOWN.]

THE SOUND OF THE SHOFAR SIGNALS THE END OF THE MEAL. THE SHOFAR MAY BE RECORDED OR LIVE. WHETHER LIVE OR RECORDED, IT IS VERY EFFECTIVE TO HAVE A COSTUMED FIGURE OF AN EARLY HEBREW PERIOD TO "BLOW" THE SHOFAR. THIS INCREASES THE IMPACT AND SIGNALS THAT THE SECOND PORTION OF THE PROGRAM IS BEGINNING AND THE AUDIENCE SHOULD RETURN TO THEIR TABLES.

FOLLOWING THE SHOFAR SOUND, THE PRIEST STANDS TO FOCUS THE ATTENTION OF THE PARTICIPANTS.]

THE FOUR QUESTIONS

SPOTLIGHT ON PRIESTLY FIGURE

PRIESTLY FIGURE: *Now it is time for the Four Questions to be read.*

SPOTLIGHT ON NARRATOR

NARRATOR: The youngest person present sits to the right of the head of the table and is the one who asks the Four Questions. The Apostle John, traditionally the youngest of the disciples, sat to Jesus' right. He was probably the one to ask the questions.

LIGHT FOR PERFORMERS

SPECIAL MUSIC - THE FOUR QUESTIONS SONG (MA NISHTANAH)

[AFTER SONG: The Child, or youngest present, asks:]

SPOTLIGHT ON CHILD

CHILD: *Why is this night different from all other nights?*

1. *On all other nights we may eat either leavened or unleavened bread, but on this night, why only unleavened bread?*

2. *On all other nights we eat herbs of any kind, but on this night, why only bitter herbs?*

3. *On all other nights, we do not dip our herbs even once; but on this night, why do we dip them twice?*

4. *On all other nights, we eat our meals sitting or reclining; but on this night, why do we eat in a reclining position?*

SPOTLIGHT ON NARRATOR

NARRATOR: DURING THE TIME OF THE TEMPLE, BEFORE A.D. 70, A DIFFERENT QUESTION WAS ASKED. BY ORDER OF ROME, FOLLOWING THE DESTRUCTION OF THE TEMPLE, LAMBS COULD NO LONGER BE SACRIFICED. THUS, THE FOURTH QUESTION WAS CHANGED TO THE ONE JUST ASKED ABOUT RECLINING; THE ANSWER HAS BEEN EXPLAINED EARLIER.

THE ORIGINAL FOURTH QUESTION WAS, "WHY DO WE EAT LAMB?" AS CHRISTIANS, WE UNDERSTAND THAT JESUS WAS THE FINAL SACRIFICE FOR ALL. THEREFORE, WE MAY ASK THE ORIGINAL QUESTION, JUST AS IT WAS ASKED THOUSANDS OF YEARS AGO.

SPOTLIGHT ON CHILD

[ASKS WHAT USED TO BE THE FOURTH QUESTION.]

CHILD: *WHY ON THIS NIGHT, DO WE SERVE AND EAT THE LAMB THAT WAS PRESENTED FOR SACRIFICE - THREE DAYS EARLIER?*

SPOTLIGHT ON PRIESTLY FIGURE

[*PRIESTLY FIGURE UNCOVERS THE MATZAH AND BEGINS THE REPLY - FIRST ADDRESSING THE YOUNG BOY BUT THEN THE ASSEMBLY.*]

BACKGROUND MUSIC UP

PRIESTLY FIGURE: *BEFORE WE READ FROM THE HAGGADAH DETAILING THE ENTIRE STORY, I WILL ANSWER YOUR QUESTIONS ONE BY ONE.*

THE ISRAELITES EAT MATZAH BECAUSE WHEN PHARAOH TOLD THEIR ANCESTORS THAT THEY COULD LEAVE EGYPT, THEY HAD NO TIME TO BAKE BREAD WITH LEAVEN, SO THEY BAKED

IT WITHOUT LEAVEN. AS CHRISTIANS, WE EAT MATZAH AS A SYMBOL OF OUR SAVIOR, JESUS CHRIST, WHO, LIKE THE MATZAH, WAS PIERCED AND STRIPED AND BECAME PAYMENT FOR THE SINS OF THE WORLD. JUST BEFORE CHRIST DIED ON THE CROSS, HE UTTERED THE GREEK PHRASE, "TE-TELES-TAI." THE WORD WAS AN OFFICIAL ACCOUNTING TERM USED AT THE TIME OF CHRIST. IT LITERALLY MEANT, "PAID IN FULL." IT WAS THIS PHRASE THAT JESUS USED AS HE WAS DYING, ANNOUNCING FROM THE CROSS, "TE-TELES-TAI." OUR DEBT OF SIN HAD BEEN PAID IN FULL.

AT THE SEDER, THE ISRAELITES EAT BITTER HERBS TO REMIND THEM OF THE BITTERNESS THEIR PREDECESSORS EXPERIENCED WHEN THEIR EGYPTIAN TASKMASTERS OPPRESSED THEM. AS CHRISTIANS, WE EAT IT TO REMIND US OF THE BITTERNESS WE EXPERIENCE WHEN THE TASKMASTER OF SIN OPPRESSES US.

AT THE SEDER, WE DIP FOOD TWICE: THE PARSLEY IS DIPPED IN SALT WATER, AS WE HAVE ALREADY EXPLAINED, AND THE MATZAH IS DIPPED INTO BITTER HERBS, AS WE WILL TELL SHORTLY.

WHEN THE JEWS LOST THEIR TEMPLE IN A.D. 70, ROME MADE IT IMPOSSIBLE FOR THEM TO CONDUCT SACRIFICES. THEREFORE, A LAMB WAS NO LONGER USED DURING PASSOVER, BECAUSE INSPECTION AND SACRIFICE OF THE LAMB WERE NOT POSSIBLE. TODAY'S MODERN JEW CONSIDERS MATZAH AS A "SUBSTITUTE" FOR THEIR SACRIFICE. LIKEWISE, CHRISTIANS CONSIDER THE MATZAH, DURING COMMUNION, AS A SUBSTITUTE FOR CHRIST, AS HE EXPLAINED DURING HIS LAST PASSOVER.

TONIGHT, AS WE EAT LAMB, WE ARE REMINDED THAT LIKE JESUS, THE LAMB OF PASSOVER WAS WITHOUT FAULT OR BLEMISH. LIKE JESUS, NO BONE WAS BROKEN. THE INNOCENT LAMB'S BLOOD COVERED THE ISRAELITES AS THE LORD STRUCK AT THE HOUSEHOLDS OF THOSE WHOSE DOORPOSTS WERE NOT COVERED BY THE BLOOD OF THE LAMB. TODAY, THE BLOOD

OF JESUS, THE LAMB OF GOD, COVERS US, SAVING US FROM THE PRICE OF SIN, SPIRITUAL DEATH.

BACKGROUND MUSIC FADES

PRIESTLY FIGURE: BLESSED IS GOD WHO GAVE THE TORAH TO HIS PEOPLE, ISRAEL. AND, BLESSED IS GOD WHO IN BLESSING ABRAHAM BLESSED THE GENTILES. BLESSED IS THE LORD.

THE FOUR SONS

SPOTLIGHT ON PRIESTLY FIGURE

PRIESTLY FIGURE: NOW WE WILL DISCUSS THE FOUR SONS.

THE TORAH DECLARES FOUR TIMES THAT A FATHER SHOULD TELL HIS SON THE STORY OF PASSOVER. RABBIS HAVE INFERRED FROM THESE SCRIPTURAL REFERENCES THAT THERE ARE FOUR TYPES OF SONS: THE WISE SON, THE REBELLIOUS SON, THE SIMPLE SON AND THE SHY SON.

BACKGROUND MUSIC UP

THE WISE SON ASKS IN DEUTERONOMY 6:20, ""WHAT IS THE MEANING OF THE LAWS AND CUSTOMS WHICH GOD HAS COMMANDED US?" SCRIPTURE SAYS TO TELL HIM ALL THE LAWS TO THE LAST DETAIL SO THAT WE ARE CAREFUL TO OBEY ALL THESE LAWS BEFORE THE LORD OUR GOD.

THE REBELLIOUS SON ASKS IN EXODUS 12:26-27 & 42, 26"AND WHEN YOUR CHILDREN SAY TO YOU, 'WHAT DOES THIS RITE MEAN TO YOU?' 27 YOU SHALL SAY, 'IT IS A PASSOVER SACRIFICE TO THE LORD WHO PASSED OVER THE HOUSES OF THE SONS OF ISRAEL IN EGYPT WHEN HE SMOTE THE EGYPTIANS BUT SPARED OUR HOMES.'" 42 IT IS A NIGHT TO BE OBSERVED FOR THE LORD FOR HAVING BROUGHT THEM OUT FROM THE LAND OF EGYPT; THIS NIGHT IS FOR THE

LORD, TO BE OBSERVED BY ALL THE SONS OF ISRAEL THROUGHOUT THEIR GENERATIONS." ONE ONLY NEEDS TO RECALL THE PUNISHMENT THE LORD EXTRACTED THOUGH THE DEATH OF 3,000 ISRAELIS WHEN THEY CAST THE IMAGE OF THE GOLDEN CALF WHILE MOSES WAS RECEIVING THE LORD'S TEN COMMANDMENTS ON MOUNT SINAI.

SPOTLIGHT ON NARRATOR

NARRATOR: LIKEWISE, HAD WE LIVED BEFORE CHRIST, WE WOULD NOT HAVE BEEN REDEEMED AS WE ARE NOW. THE PASSOVER SERVICE REMINDS US THAT THIS WAS GOD'S PLAN FOR MANKIND FROM THE TIME ADAM AND EVE WERE FORCED FROM THE GARDEN UNTIL THE BIRTH, DEATH, AND RESURRECTION OF JESUS CHRIST.

SPOTLIGHT ON PRIESTLY FIGURE

PRIESTLY FIGURE: THE SIMPLE SON ASKS IN EXODUS 13:14, "...'WHAT IS THIS?' THEN YOU SHALL SAY TO HIM, 'WITH A POWERFUL HAND THE LORD BROUGHT US OUT OF EGYPT, FROM THE HOUSE OF SLAVERY.'"

SPOTLIGHT ON NARRATOR

NARRATOR: JESUS EXPRESSED IT SO WELL IN JOHN 14:1, WHEN HE SAID, "LET NOT YOUR HEART BE TROUBLED. TRUST IN GOD; TRUST ALSO IN ME."

SPOTLIGHT ON PRIESTLY FIGURE

PRIESTLY FIGURE: AS FOR THE SHY SON, WHO DOES NOT EVEN KNOW HOW TO ASK, YOU MUST BEGIN FOR HIM. AS IT IS WRITTEN IN THE TORAH, "YOU SHALL TELL YOUR CHILD ON THAT DAY: 'I DO THIS BECAUSE OF WHAT THE LORD DID FOR ME, WHEN I CAME OUT OF EGYPT.'" THUS, ONE MUST AROUSE HIS INTEREST IN WHAT THE LORD HAS AND WILL DO.

SPOTLIGHT ON NARRATOR

NARRATOR: As CHRISTIANS, WE PARTICIPATE IN PASSOVER, REMEMBERING THAT LOVE STORY WRITTEN IN BLOOD ON A WOODEN CROSS, TWO THOUSAND YEARS AGO, IN A LAND CALLED JUDEA.

SPOTLIGHT ON PRIESTLY FIGURE

BACKGROUND MUSIC FADES

PRIESTLY FIGURE: BLESSED IS GOD, WHO KEEPS HIS PROMISES TO ISRAEL AND TO US. BLESSED IS HE.

MAGGID (TELLING THE PASSOVER STORY)

RESPONSIVE READING:

SPOTLIGHT ON NARRATOR

NARRATOR: IN YOUR SEDER PROGRAM, PLEASE TURN TO THE SECTION TITLED "THE PASSOVER STORY."

SPOTLIGHT MAINTAINED ON PRIESTLY FIGURE AND NARRATOR DURING RESPONSIVE READING

LOW BACKGROUND MUSIC UP

PRIESTLY FIGURE: NOW WE WILL READ THE TELLING OF THE PASSOVER STORY RESPONSIVELY FROM THE SEDER PROGRAM.

THE BIBLE TEACHES THAT DURING A GREAT FAMINE IN THE LAND OF CANAAN, THE SONS OF JACOB, WHOSE NAME HAD BEEN CHANGED TO ISRAEL, JOURNEYED TO EGYPT TO PURCHASE FOOD FROM THE PHARAOH. THERE THEY WERE REUNITED WITH THEIR BROTHER JOSEPH. BECAUSE OF HIS INFLUENCE, THEY WERE PERMITTED TO DWELL IN THE FERTILE PLAINS OF GOSHEN. AT FIRST, THE HOUSE OF ISRAEL

NUMBERED FEWER THAN 80 PEOPLE. BUT IN TIME, THEIR NUMBERS EXPANDED, THEIR FLOCKS INCREASED, AND THEY BECAME A NATION.

NOTE: NARRATOR LEADS ATTENDEES IN THE RESPONSIVE READING.

ALL: AND THEN THERE AROSE A NEW PHARAOH, ONE WHO DID NOT KNOW JOSEPH. HE BEHELD THE MIGHT OF ISRAEL, AND HE FEARED THAT IN TIME OF WAR THE SONS OF JACOB MIGHT ALIGN THEMSELVES WITH EGYPT'S FOES.

PRIESTLY FIGURE: AND SO, HE SUBDUED THE ISRAELITES, AND HE AFFLICTED THEM WITH CRUEL LABOR. TASKMASTERS WERE PLACED OVER THE ISRAELITES, TO COMPEL THEM TO MAKE BRICKS AND TO BUILD PHARAOH'S CITIES.

ALL: BUT DESPITE THEIR HARDSHIP, ISRAEL CONTINUED TO THRIVE, JUST AS GOD HAD PROMISED. THIS CAUSED PHARAOH EVEN GREATER ALARM, AND HE ORDERED THE SLAUGHTER OF ISRAEL'S INFANT SONS. BY HIS COMMAND, EVERY MALE CHILD BORN TO THE HEBREWS WAS TO BE CAST INTO THE NILE AND DROWNED.

PRIESTLY FIGURE: HOW TERRIBLE WAS THE SUFFERING OF THE ISRAELITES. IN ANGUISH, THEY CRIED TO THE GOD OF ABRAHAM, ISAAC, AND JACOB. AND GOD HEARD THEIR CRY AND REMEMBERED HIS COVENANT. HE RAISED UP A DELIVERER, A REDEEMER, THE MAN MOSES. HE SENT MOSES TO PHARAOH'S COURT TO DECLARE THE COMMANDMENT OF THE LORD.

ALL: LET MY PEOPLE GO.

PRIESTLY FIGURE: BUT PHARAOH WOULD NOT LISTEN TO THE WORD OF GOD. SO, MOSES PRONOUNCED GOD'S JUDGMENT ON PHARAOH'S HOUSE AND ON PHARAOH'S

LAND. PLAGUES WERE POURED OUT UPON THE EGYPTIANS, UPON THEIR CROPS, AND UPON THEIR FLOCKS.

ALL: BUT PHARAOH'S HEART WAS HARDENED. HE WOULD NOT YIELD TO THE WILL OF GOD. HE WOULD NOT LET THE HOUSE OF JACOB DEPART.

PRIESTLY FIGURE: *THEN THE TENTH PLAGUE FELL UPON THE LAND OF EGYPT: THE DEATH OF EGYPT'S FIRSTBORN. "AS THE PHARAOH HAD SLAIN THE INNOCENT CHILDREN OF GOD'S CHOSEN PEOPLE, SO NOW THE LORD TOOK THE FIRSTBORN IN THE LAND OF EGYPT, FROM THE FIRSTBORN OF PHARAOH WHO SAT UPON HIS THRONE, TO THE FIRSTBORN OF THE MAID SERVANT WHO WAS BEHIND THE MILL AND ALL THE FIRSTBORN OF BEASTS...AND AGAINST ALL THE GODS OF EGYPT DID GOD EXECUTE HIS JUDGMENT." BUT TO PROTECT THE CHILDREN OF ISRAEL, GOD COMMANDED THE HEAD OF EACH JEWISH HOUSEHOLD TO SACRIFICE A SPOTLESS LAMB, WITHOUT BREAKING ANY OF ITS BONES, AND TO APPLY ITS BLOOD TO THE DOORWAY OF THEIR HOMES, FIRST TO THE TOP OF THE DOORWAY, THE LINTEL, AND THEN TO THE TWO SIDE POSTS.*

ALL: AND THE BLOOD SHALL BE TO YOU FOR A TOKEN UPON THE HOUSES WHERE YOU ARE; AND WHEN I SEE THE BLOOD, I WILL PASS OVER YOU, AND THE PLAGUES SHALL NOT BE UPON YOU TO DESTROY YOU WHEN I SMITE THE LAND OF EGYPT.

PRIESTLY FIGURE: *BY THE BLOOD OF THE LAMB WAS ISRAEL SPARED.*

ALL: BY THE BLOOD OF THE LAMB WAS JACOB REDEEMED. BY THE BLOOD OF THE LAMB WAS DEATH MADE TO PASS OVER. WITHOUT THE BLOOD, THERE WAS DEATH. WITH THE BLOOD, THERE IS LIFE.

PRIESTLY FIGURE: *We recognize this prophetic parallel. We also recognize the symbol that was drawn by the blood on the entrance to the house. This symbol was written over the Hebrew homes nearly 1500 years before the birth of Christ. It is the symbol of the cross.*

ALL: Just as the blood of those first Passover lambs was applied in faith to the doorposts of Israel's homes, so the blood of the Messiah must be applied in faith to the doorposts of our hearts.

SPOTLIGHT OFF NARRATOR

PRIESTLY FIGURE: *Tonight, we worship God not only because the Lord passed over the homes of the Israelites, but because, all of us, whether Jew or Gentile, may be redeemed from even greater bondage through our faith in the Messiah of Israel and the world, the Messiah Jesus. Through Him, we may pass over from death to life, "saved by the Blood of the Lamb."*

BACKGROUND MUSIC FADES

THE SECOND CUP (PLAGUES AND INIQUITY)

PRIESTLY FIGURE: *Lift the Second Cup, "the Cup of Plagues and Iniquity."*

God's promise to Adam, Noah, Abraham, Isaac, and Jacob holds true for us, too! For more than once has the enemy of God risen up to destroy us. But the Holy One, blessed be He, the Lord our God, saves us!

SPOTLIGHT ON NARRATOR

NARRATOR: PLEASE RAISE YOUR CUP IN A TOAST - BUT THEN REPLACE IT ON THE TABLE.

[ATTENDEES TOAST, THEN PUT DOWN THE CUP.]

THE TEN PLAGUES

SPOTLIGHT ON PRIESTLY FIGURE

PRIESTLY FIGURE: THE TEN PLAGUES REMIND US THAT OUR JOY CANNOT BE COMPLETE BECAUSE OUR OWN REDEMPTION INVOLVED SUFFERING. THE REDEMPTION OF THE ISRAELITES CAME AT THE SUFFERING OF THE EGYPTIANS.

[PRIESTLY FIGURE RAISES THE CUP AND SAYS-]

A FULL CUP IS A SYMBOL OF JOY, AND WE REJOICE TONIGHT. BUT WE SHALL NOW DIMINISH OUR CUP - TO SHOW THAT OUR JOY IS NOT COMPLETE. AS CHRISTIANS, OUR JOY CANNOT BE COMPLETE SO LONG AS SO MANY REMAIN IN BONDAGE - TO SIN.

THESE WERE THE **TEN PLAGUES,** WHICH THE HOLY ONE, PRAISED BE HE, BROUGHT UPON THE EGYPTIANS. I WILL FIRST SAY THE PLAGUES IN HEBREW, AND THEN TOGETHER WE WILL ALL REPEAT THE PLAGUES IN ENGLISH. AS THE PLAGUES ARE SPOKEN IN ENGLISH, WE WILL EACH DIMINISH OUR CUP BY ONE DROP FOR EACH PLAGUE AS IT IS SPOKEN.

[A CYMBAL SOUNDS FOR EACH PLAGUE AS IT IS READ.]

1	DAHM	5	DEH-VER	9	KHO-SHEKH
2	TZFAR-DAY-AH	6	SH'KHEEN	10	MAHKAT B'AKH-ROTE
3	KEE-NEEM	7	BAH-RODE		
4	AH-ROV	8	AR-BEH		

PROVERBS 24:17 SAYS, "DO NOT REJOICE WHEN YOUR ENEMY FALLS, AND DO NOT LET YOUR HEART BE GLAD WHEN HE STUMBLES." JUST AS THE HEBREW PEOPLE REDUCED THEIR FULL CUP OF JOY BY A DROP FOR EACH OF THE TEN PLAGUES, SO WE WILL DO LIKEWISE.

WITH YOUR LITTLE FINGER DIP INTO YOUR CUP TO REMOVE A DROP, ONE FOR EACH OF THE PLAGUES, PLACING IT ONTO YOUR PLATE [NAPKIN]. REPEAT, AFTER ME.

[A CYMBAL SOUNDS FOR EACH PLAGUE AS IT IS READ ALOUD.]

SPOTLIGHT ON NARRATOR ALONG WITH PRIESTLY FIGURE

ALL: BLOOD, FROGS, LICE, SWARMS OF INSECTS, CATTLE DISEASE, BOILS, HAIL, LOCUSTS, DARKNESS, SLAYING OF THE FIRSTBORN.

SPOTLIGHT OFF NARRATOR

DAYEINU ("ENOUGH FOR US")

PRIESTLY FIGURE: IT IS TIME FOR "DAYEINU." HOW THANKFUL MUST WE BE TO GOD, THE ALL-KNOWING, ALL-LOVING ONE, FOR ALL THE GOOD HE HAS DONE FOR US! FOR EACH BLESSING, WE GIVE THANKS!

SPOTLIGHT ON NARRATOR AND PRIESTLY FIGURE FOR READING

NARRATOR: TRADITIONALLY, THE JEWS HAVE PRAISED GOD FOR THEIR BLESSINGS OF DELIVERANCE FROM BONDAGE. WHILE WE WERE NOT IN EGYPT, IT IS INSTRUCTIVE TO HEAR THE JEWISH WORDS OF SUFFICIENCY. THEIR WORDS CONTAIN HUMILITY FROM WHICH WE ALL MAY LEARN. FOR EXAMPLE, "IF GOD HAD ONLY DELIVERED US FROM EGYPT, IT WOULD HAVE BEEN ENOUGH FOR US. IT WOULD HAVE BEEN SUFFICIENT."

THE HEBREW WORD FOR THE EXPRESSION, "IT WOULD HAVE BEEN ENOUGH" IS "**DAYEINU**," PRONOUNCED: **DIE-AY-NU.** PLEASE SAY IT WITH ME.

ALL: DAYEINU

NARRATOR: YOU WILL SAY THIS WORD AFTER EACH OF THE FOLLOWING STATEMENTS.

BACKGROUND MUSIC UP

PRIESTLY FIGURE: *HAD HE BROUGHT US OUT FROM EGYPT AND NOT EXECUTED JUDGMENT AGAINST THEM.*

ALL: DAYEINU

PRIESTLY FIGURE: *HAD HE EXECUTED JUDGMENT AGAINST THEM AND NOT DONE JUSTICE TO THEIR IDOLS.*

ALL: DAYEINU

PRIESTLY FIGURE: *HAD HE DONE JUSTICE TO THEIR IDOLS AND NOT SLAIN THEIR FIRSTBORN.*

ALL: DAYEINU

PRIESTLY FIGURE: *HAD HE SLAIN THEIR FIRSTBORN AND NOT GIVEN US THEIR PROPERTY.*

ALL: DAYEINU

PRIESTLY FIGURE: *HAD HE GIVEN US THEIR PROPERTY AND NOT DIVIDED THE SEA FOR US.*

ALL: DAYEINU

PRIESTLY FIGURE: *THERE ARE MANY, MANY VERSES IN THE ORTHODOX HAGGADAH, BUT WE WILL SAY "DAYEINU" AT FIVE.*

THE 22ND VERSE IN THE MOST ANCIENT ORTHODOX HAGGADAH GIVES THANKS FOR THE TEMPLE TO ATONE FOR SIN. BUT SINCE ITS DESTRUCTION, WHERE DOES ONE TURN FOR ATONEMENT TODAY? JESUS ANSWERED THE QUESTION WHEN IN JOHN 2:19 HE SAID, "...DESTROY THIS TEMPLE, AND IN THREE DAYS I WILL RAISE IT UP." HE WAS SPEAKING OF THE TEMPLE OF HIS BODY.

IT WOULD HAVE BEEN ENOUGH FOR US IF THROUGH JESUS WE RECEIVED ETERNAL SALVATION AND NOT RECEIVED HIS HOLY SPIRIT; IT WOULD HAVE BEEN ENOUGH FOR US.

ALL: DAYEINU

PRIESTLY FIGURE: *HAD HE GIVEN US HIS HOLY SPIRIT AND NOT BESTOWED US WITH THE FRUIT OF THE SPIRIT; IT WOULD HAVE BEEN ENOUGH FOR US.*

ALL: DAYEINU

PRIESTLY FIGURE: *HAD HE BESTOWED US WITH THE FRUIT OF THE SPIRIT AND NOT GIVEN US HIS PEACE, IT WOULD HAVE BEEN ENOUGH FOR US.*

ALL: DAYEINU

BACKGROUND MUSIC FADES

PRIESTLY FIGURE: *LET US SING FOR JOY TO OUR LORD!*

LIGHT FOR PERFORMERS ONLY

SING DAYEINU SONG

SPOTLIGHT ON PRIESTLY FIGURE

PRIESTLY FIGURE: *IN EVERY GENERATION, ONE MUST LOOK UPON HIMSELF AS THOUGH HE PERSONALLY HAD COME OUT FROM EGYPT, FOR IT IS GOD WHO LEADS US FROM TURMOIL IN TIMES OF TROUBLE. IT IS HE, WHO PLEDGED THROUGH JESUS CHRIST, SALVATION FOR ALL WHO COME TO HIM.*

AS IT SAYS IN ROMANS, "6KNOWING THIS, THAT OUR OLD SELF WAS CRUCIFIED WITH HIM, IN ORDER THAT OUR BODY OF SIN MIGHT BE DONE AWAY WITH, SO THAT WE WOULD NO LONGER BE SLAVES TO SIN; "8NOW IF WE HAVE DIED WITH CHRIST, WE BELIEVE THAT WE SHALL ALSO LIVE WITH HIM. "11EVEN SO CONSIDER YOURSELVES TO BE DEAD TO SIN, BUT ALIVE TO GOD IN CHRIST JESUS."

[PRIESTLY FIGURE RAISES THE CUP AND SAYS:]

PRIESTLY FIGURE: *THEREFORE, IT IS OUR DUTY TO THANK AND PRAISE IN SONG AND PRAYER, TO GLORIFY AND WORSHIP HIM WHO PERFORMED ALL THE WONDERS FOR THE ISRAELITES - AND FOR US. HE BROUGHT US FROM THE SLAVERY OF SIN TO THE FREEDOM OF SALVATION ... FROM ANGUISH TO JOY ... FROM SORROW TO FESTIVITY, AND FROM DARKNESS TO LIGHT.*

SPOTLIGHT ON NARRATOR

NARRATOR: EVERYONE NOW, PLEASE RAISE YOUR SECOND CUP; DON'T DRINK, BUT PREPARE TO DO SO!

SPOTLIGHT ON PRIESTLY FIGURE

PRIESTLY FIGURE: *NOW IS THE TIME FOR THE DRINKING OF THE SECOND CUP, THE CUP OF PLAGUES.*

BA-ROOK AH-TAH AH-DOH-NAI EL-OHAY-NU MEL-ICK HA-OH-LAM BORAY P'RIE HA GAW-FEN

[REPEATS IN ENGLISH]

BLESSED ART THOU, O LORD OUR GOD, RULER OF THE UNIVERSE, CREATOR OF THE FRUIT OF THE VINE.

SPOTLIGHT ON NARRATOR AND PRIESTLY FIGURE

NARRATOR: EVERYONE LEAN SLIGHTLY TO YOUR LEFT AND DRINK THE SECOND CUP.

[ALL DRINK THE SECOND CUP, LEANING TO THE LEFT.]

BAREICH (GRACE AFTER THE MEAL)

SPOTLIGHT ON NARRATOR AND PRIESTLY FIGURE

PRIESTLY FIGURE: *NOW IS THE BAREICH, THE GRACE AFTER THE MEAL.*

BACKGROUND MUSIC UP

NARRATOR: LET US CONTINUE THE SEDER BY READING RESPONSIVELY FROM THE HAGGADAH.

PRIESTLY FIGURE: *LET US GIVE THANKS TO THE LORD.*

ALL: MAY THE NAME OF THE LORD BE BLESSED FROM THIS TIME FORTH AND FOREVER.

PRIESTLY FIGURE: *WE PRAISE YOU, O GOD, FROM WHOSE ABUNDANCE WE HAVE PARTAKEN.*

ALL: WE PRAISE YOU, O LORD OUR GOD, OUR SAVIOR AND OUR KING, WHO GIVES BREAD TO ALL FLESH, FOR YOUR LOVING-KINDNESS ENDURE FOREVER.

NARRATOR: EVERYONE, PLEASE FILL YOUR CUP NOW, IN PREPARATION FOR THE "CUP OF REDEMPTION."

SPOTLIGHT OFF NARRATOR

TZAFON *(EATING OF THE AFIKOMEN)*

PRIESTLY FIGURE: *NOW FOR TZAFON, THE EATING OF THE AFIKOMEN. THE MEAL CANNOT BE COMPLETED WITHOUT EATING THE AFIKOMEN. THE AFIKOMEN IS THE BROKEN MIDDLE MATZAH THAT WAS HIDDEN. IT MUST BE FOUND AND BROUGHT BACK. THE CHILD WHO FINDS IT RECEIVES A GREAT REWARD.*

SPOTLIGHT ON NARRATOR

NARRATOR: ALL CHILDREN MUST NOW GET UP AND FIND THE AFIKOMEN, WHICH HAS ALREADY BEEN HIDDEN. NO ONE CAN LEAVE UNTIL IT IS LOCATED.

> *["WARM/COLD" HINTS ARE OKAY TO HELP THE CHILDREN. WHEN THE AFIKOMEN IS FOUND, AND RETURNED, THE REWARD IS GIVEN BY THE HONORED WIFE, AND THE SERVICE CONTINUES.]*

SPOTLIGHT ON PRIESTLY FIGURE

BACKGROUND MUSIC FADES

PRIESTLY FIGURE: *THE MATZAH, WHICH COVERED THE SMALL, CEREMONIAL LAST PIECE OF PASSOVER LAMB, WAS THE LAST ITEM EATEN AT THE SEDER. THIS COMBINATION OF BITTER HERBS, MATZAH, AND LAMB, EMPHASIZED THE SIGNIFICANCE OF THE MATZAH.*

AFTER JERUSALEM FELL IN A.D. 70, A LAMB WAS NO LONGER EATEN AT THE SEDER, AND THE AFIKOMEN ALONE BECAME REPRESENTATIVE OF THE LAMB - AND AN ELEMENT OF THE CHRISTIAN COMMUNION SERVICE.

THE APOSTLE JOHN SAID IT WELL WHEN HE WROTE IN JOHN 1:29, "BEHOLD, THE LAMB OF GOD WHO TAKES AWAY THE SIN OF THE WORLD!"

LIGHT FOR PERFORMERS

SPECIAL MUSIC - COMMUNION SONG

SPOTLIGHT ON PRIESTLY FIGURE

PRIESTLY FIGURE: *IT WAS DURING THE BLESSING AFTER THE MEAL AND THE EATING OF THE AFIKOMEN THAT THE BIBLE TELLS US IN 1ST CORINTHIANS, "JESUS, THE SAME NIGHT IN WHICH HE WAS BETRAYED, TOOK BREAD: AND WHEN HE HAD GIVEN THANKS, HE BROKE IT, AND SAID, 'TAKE, EAT: THIS IS MY BODY, WHICH IS BROKEN FOR YOU, THIS DO IN REMEMBRANCE OF ME.'"*

SPOTLIGHT ON NARRATOR

NARRATOR: IT IS FROM THIS PART OF THE PASSOVER SERVICE THAT WE COMMEMORATE COMMUNION. EACH PERSON SHOULD NOW TAKE A PORTION OF THE BREAD AS IT

IS BEING PASSED AT YOUR TABLE. PLEASE PASS THE BREAD FROM LEFT TO RIGHT.

[EACH PERSON IS GIVEN A PORTION OF THE BREAD, AS IT IS PASSED]

SPOTLIGHT ON PRIESTLY FIGURE

PRIESTLY FIGURE: JESUS SAID IN JOHN 6:35, "I AM THE BREAD OF LIFE. HE WHO COMES TO ME WILL NEVER GO HUNGRY, AND HE WHO BELIEVES IN ME WILL NEVER BE THIRSTY."

THE APOSTLE PAUL WROTE IN 1ST CORINTHIANS, SAYING, "7 A MAN OUGHT TO EXAMINE HIMSELF BEFORE HE EATS OF THE BREAD AND DRINKS OF THE CUP."

LET US PAUSE FOR A MOMENT OF REFLECTION AND EXAMINATION.

[PAUSE]

NOW, LET US EAT THE BREAD. HIS SACRIFICIAL DEATH ON THE CROSS FULFILLED THE PROPHETIC SYMBOLISM OF THE PASSOVER LAMB.

THE THIRD CUP (THE CUP OF REDEMPTION)

SPOTLIGHT ON PRIESTLY FIGURE

PRIESTLY FIGURE: NOW IT IS TIME FOR THE THIRD CUP, WHICH IS THE "CUP OF REDEMPTION."

BACKGROUND MUSIC UP

PRIESTLY FIGURE: IT WAS WITH THIS CUP THE WORD OF GOD IN LUKE 22:20 TELLS US, "AND IN THE SAME WAY HE

261

TOOK THE CUP AFTER THEY HAD EATEN, SAYING, "THIS CUP WHICH IS POURED OUT FOR YOU IS THE NEW COVENANT IN MY BLOOD.'"

SPOTLIGHT ON NARRATOR

NARRATOR: PLEASE BOW YOUR HEADS FOR A MOMENT OF PERSONAL PRAYER AND SILENT CONTEMPLATION.

[PERSONAL PRAYER - PAUSE FOR MOMENTS OF SILENT PRAYER AND CONTEMPLATION]

SPOTLIGHT ON PRIESTLY FIGURE

PRIESTLY FIGURE: I WILL LIFT UP THE CUP OF SALVATION, THE CUP OF YASHUA, AND CALL ON THE NAME OF THE LORD. REMEMBERING THAT JESUS' BLOOD WAS POURED OUT FOR THE FORGIVENESS OF SINS, LET US BE THANKFUL.

BLESSED ART THOU, O LORD, OUR GOD, KING OF THE UNIVERSE, CREATOR OF THE FRUIT OF THE VINE. LET US DRINK THE CUP.

SPOTLIGHT ON NARRATOR

NARRATOR: EVERYONE LIFT AND DRINK THE THIRD CUP.

[ALL DRINK THE THIRD CUP]

SPOTLIGHT ON PRIESTLY FIGURE

PRIESTLY FIGURE: THE APOSTLE PAUL WROTE OF THIS CUP AND BREAD IN 1ST CORINTHIANS 10:16 & 11:26, "IS NOT THE CUP OF THANKSGIVING FOR WHICH WE GIVE THANKS TO PARTICIPATION IN THE BLOOD OF CHRIST? AND IS NOT THE BREAD THAT WE BREAK A PARTICIPATION IN THE BODY OF CHRIST?" "26 FOR AS OFTEN AS YOU EAT THIS BREAD AND

DRINK THE CUP, YOU PROCLAIM THE LORD'S DEATH UNTIL HE COMES."

SPOTLIGHT ON NARRATOR

NARRATOR: IT WAS BY GOD'S GRACE AND FOR HIS NAME'S SAKE THAT ISRAEL WAS REDEEMED, BUT NOT BY THEIR OWN RIGHTEOUSNESS. SO, IT IS ALSO WITH OUR REDEMPTION FROM SIN AND SPIRITUAL DEATH. IT IS NOT BY WORKS BUT BY FAITH IN GOD.

WE ARE WITNESSES TO GOD'S POWER TO DELIVER US FROM SLAVERY AND SIN. GOD CALLS US OUT. JUST AS GOD DID NOT WANT THE ISRAELITES TO LOOK LONGINGLY BACK TO THE DAYS OF BONDAGE IN EGYPT, WE ARE NOT TO LOOK LONGINGLY BACK TO THE DAYS OF BONDAGE TO SIN.

WE HAVE PARTAKEN OF THE AFIKOMEN AND THE THIRD CUP OF REDEMPTION, REMEMBERING THE ONE WHO WAS TO COME HAS ALREADY COME AND WILL COME AGAIN.

JEWS AND CHRISTIANS HAVE A BELIEF THAT IS IN COMMON WITH EACH OTHER, YET WITH THIS DIFFERENCE: THE TORAH-BASED JEW BELIEVES THE MESSIAH IS YET TO COME; THE TORAH-BASED CHRISTIAN BELIEVES THAT HE IS TO COME AGAIN, THIS TIME AS "MESHACH BEN DAH-VEED," TRANSLATED AS "THE MESSIAH, SON OF DAVID."

YASHUA'S GENEALOGY, SHOWN IN THE TEMPLE RECORDS, CLEARLY DEMONSTRATED THAT HE IS FROM THE LINE OF DAVID. THOSE RECORDS WERE DESTROYED BY THE ROMANS AND NO LONGER EXIST. CONSEQUENTLY, ANYONE FOLLOWING WHO CLAIMED TO BE THE MESSIAH COULD NOT FULFILL THE GENEALOGY REQUIRED BY PROPHECY AS HAD JESUS. THEREFORE, NO ONE IN THIS AGE NEED APPLY FOR THE POSITION. HOWEVER, IN THAT DAY – MAY WE ALL UNITE UNDER THE SINGLE BANNER OF YASHUA, MESSIAH THE KING.

BACKGROUND MUSIC FADES

SPOTLIGHT ON PRIESTLY FIGURE

PRIESTLY FIGURE: *PLEASE FILL YOUR FOURTH CUP, THE CUP OF "THANKSGIVING AND COMPLETION – THE CUP OF ELIJAH"!*

POURING THE FOURTH CUP
(ELIJAH, THE PROPHET)

SPOTLIGHT ON PRIESTLY FIGURE

PRIESTLY FIGURE: *NOW THAT YOU HAVE FILLED THE FOURTH CUP, ALSO CALLED, "THE CUP OF ELIJAH," PLEASE RAISE IT. NOW IF SOMEONE WILL OPEN THE FRONT DOOR, EVERYONE ELSE SHOULD PLEASE RISE.*

ELIJAH IS THE BEARER OF GOOD TIDINGS OF JOY AND PEACE. HIS NAME IS UNIQUELY ASSOCIATED WITH THE COMING OF THE MESSIAH, WHOSE ADVENT HE IS EXPECTED TO ANNOUNCE.

SPOTLIGHT ON CHILD

CHILD: *FROM MALACHI 4:5-6, "I WILL SEND YOU THE PROPHET ELIJAH BEFORE THAT GREAT AND DREADFUL DAY OF THE LORD COMES. HE WILL TURN THE HEARTS OF THE FATHERS TO THEIR CHILDREN, AND THE HEARTS OF THE CHILDREN TO THEIR FATHERS."*

BACKGROUND MUSIC UP

SPOTLIGHT ON NARRATOR

NARRATOR: JEWISH LEGEND DECLARES THAT ELIJAH VISITS EVERY JEWISH HOME AT THE SEDER AND SIPS FROM THE CUP. WHEN ISRAEL WAS EXILED FROM THE LAND, THE CUP OF ELIJAH WAS FILLED, BUT NOT DRUNK. IT REMAINS ON THE TABLE AS A SIGN OF GOD'S FURTHER MESSIANIC PROMISE OF RENEWAL.

SPOTLIGHT ON PRIESTLY FIGURE

PRIESTLY FIGURE: WE RECALL JESUS' SAYING OF JOHN THE BAPTIST, IN MARK 9:11-13, 11"THEY ASKED HIM, SAYING, 'WHY IS IT THAT THE SCRIBES SAY THAT ELIJAH MUST COME FIRST?' 12AND HE SAID TO THEM, 'ELIJAH DOES FIRST COME AND RESTORE ALL THINGS. AND YET HOW IS IT WRITTEN OF THE SON OF MAN THAT HE WILL SUFFER MANY THINGS AND BE TREATED WITH CONTEMPT? 13"BUT I SAY TO YOU THAT ELIJAH HAS INDEED COME, AND THEY DID TO HIM WHATEVER THEY WISHED, JUST AS IT IS WRITTEN OF HIM.'

ELIJAH HAS COME! THIS WAS INDEED TRUE IN THE PERSON OF JOHN THE BAPTIZER. THEREFORE, THERE IS NO NEED TO OPEN THE DOOR AND LOOK FOR HIS ARRIVAL. SO PLEASE CLOSE THE DOOR AND BE SEATED. ELIJAH AND THE MESSIAH HAVE ALREADY COME, AND WE AWAIT HIS RETURN.

[THE DOOR IS CLOSED]

PRIESTLY FIGURE: LET US PRAY FOR THE PEACE OF JERUSALEM.

BACKGROUND MUSIC FADES

HALLEL
(PSALMS OF PRAISE)

SPOTLIGHT ON PRIESTLY FIGURE

PRIESTLY FIGURE: *We come now to the Hallel or Psalms of Praise.*

SPOTLIGHT ON NARRATOR

NARRATOR: Psalms 113 to 118 are Passover Psalms. The Great Passover Hallel is Psalm 136. The temple choir sang these in the temple during Passover.

Please follow along responsively the "Hallel" of Praise from Psalm 118.

SPOTLIGHT ON PRIESTLY FIGURE AND NARRATOR FOR RESPONSIVE READING

PRIESTLY FIGURE: *Praise the Lord!*

BACKGROUND MUSIC UP

ALL: Give thanks to the LORD, for He is good; For His loving-kindness is everlasting.

PRIESTLY FIGURE: *Let Israel say: His love endures forever.*

ALL: Oh let the house of Aaron say, "His loving-kindness is everlasting."

PRIESTLY FIGURE: *Let those who fear the LORD say: His love endures forever.*

ALL: I shall give thanks to You, for You have answered me, And You have become my salvation. The stone, which the builders rejected, has become the chief corner stone.

PRIESTLY FIGURE: GIVE THANKS TO THE LORD, FOR HE IS GOOD; HIS LOVE ENDURES FOREVER. AMEN.

AND NOW, LET US DECLARE SO THAT ALL MAY HEAR, THAT JESUS CHRIST IS OUR LORD AND SAVIOR AND IS THE SON OF THE LIVING GOD. IT IS IN HIM THAT WE PLACE OUR ETERNAL HOPE AND OUR SALVATION.

ALL: JESUS CHRIST IS OUR LORD AND SAVIOR AND IS THE SON OF THE LIVING GOD. IT IS IN HIM THAT WE PLACE OUR ETERNAL HOPE AND OUR SALVATION.

BACKGROUND MUSIC FADES

PRIESTLY FIGURE: BLESSED IS THE ONE WHO COMES IN THE NAME OF THE LORD.

ALL: GIVE THANKS TO THE LORD, FOR HE IS GOOD; FOR HIS LOVING-KINDNESS IS EVERLASTING.

LIGHT FOR PERFORMERS

OPTIONAL: CONGREGATIONAL SONG OF PRAISE (HALLEL)

DRINKING THE CUP OF TAKING OUT

SPOTLIGHT ON NARRATOR

NARRATOR: THE FOURTH CUP, CALLED "THE CUP OF TAKING OUT," IS THE ONE MANY SCHOLARS BELIEVE JESUS DID NOT COMPLETE. MATTHEW QUOTES CHRIST AS SAYING, "I TELL YOU, I WILL NOT DRINK OF THIS FRUIT OF THE VINE FROM NOW ON UNTIL THAT DAY WHEN I DRINK IT ANEW WITH YOU IN MY FATHER'S KINGDOM." AND AGAIN, IN LUKE, "FOR I TELL YOU I WILL NOT DRINK AGAIN FROM THE FRUIT OF THE VINE UNTIL THE KINGDOM OF GOD COMES."

267

PLEASE RAISE YOUR FOURTH CUP, THE "CUP OF PRAISE AND COMPLETION." AS JESUS, DID NOT DRINK OF THIS CUP, WE WILL NOT DRINK OF IT, EITHER INSTEAD, WE WILL AWAIT HIS RETURN.

SPOTLIGHT ON PRIESTLY FIGURE

[THE CUP IS SET UPON THE TABLE.]

PRIESTLY FIGURE: *BA-ROOK AH-TAH AH-DOH-NAI EL-O-HAY-NU MEL-ICK HA-OH-LAHM BORAY P'REE HA GAW-FEN. AMAIN*

BLESSED ART THOU, O LORD OUR GOD, RULER OF THE UNIVERSE, CREATOR OF THE FRUIT OF THE VINE.

AT THE TIME OF THE LAST SUPPER, MARK RECORDED THAT "WHEN THEY HAD SUNG A HYMN, THEY WENT OUT TO THE MOUNT OF OLIVES. 'YOU WILL ALL FALL AWAY,' JESUS TOLD THEM, 'FOR IT IS WRITTEN: "I WILL STRIKE THE SHEPHERD, AND THE SHEEP WILL BE SCATTERED." BUT AFTER I HAVE RISEN, I WILL GO AHEAD OF YOU INTO GALILEE.'"

JESUS, AFTER SINGING AND CLOSING THE PASSOVER DINNER, HAD TO LEAVE THE CITY, FOR THE ATONEMENT LAMB'S BODY WAS ALWAYS OFFERED UP TO GOD OUTSIDE THE CITY'S WALLS.

NARRATOR: *AS WAS RECORDED IN THE GOSPELS, JESUS WENT OUTSIDE OF THE WALLS OF JERUSALEM TO PRAY. IT WAS THERE, JUST AS THE PASSOVER LAMB WAS OFFERED UP, THAT THE TEMPLE GUARD OUTSIDE THE CITY'S WALLS SEIZED JESUS WHERE HE WAS TO CONTINUE UPON THE REDEMPTIVE PATH THAT GOD HAD PREPARED TO FREE HIS PEOPLE FROM SIN.*

[IF THE OPTIONAL SONG IS INCLUDED, THE PRIESTLY FIGURE SAYS -]

PRIESTLY FIGURE: LET US SING TO THE LORD!

A SONG OF PRAISE & WORSHIP (OPTIONAL)

NIRTZAH (CONCLUSION OF THE SEDER)

BACKGROUND MUSIC UP

PRIESTLY FIGURE: THE NIRTZAH IS THE CONCLUSION OF THE SEDER. IN CLOSING, LET US BOW OUR HEADS IN PRAYER AS WE CALL OUT TO OUR GOD WHO IS OUR LORD AND SAVIOR.

HAVE COMPASSION, O LORD OUR GOD, UPON US, YOUR SERVANTS. WE PRAY FOR OUR NATION, ITS LEADERS AND ITS PEOPLE; FOR OUR CHURCH, ITS MEMBERS AND ITS MINISTERS. WE PRAY THAT OUR NATION'S LEADERS WILL BE COMPELLED TO BLESS ISRAEL. WE PRAY FOR ISRAEL AND JERUSALEM, YOUR HOLY CITY. WE PRAY FOR THE REBUILDING OF THAT NATION AND THE RESTORATION OF ITS PEOPLE. WE ALSO PRAY FOR THAT TIME WHEN YOU SHALL RETURN FOR YOUR CHURCH, AND FOR THAT FINAL MOMENT, WHEN ALL MEN AND WOMEN, JEW AND GENTILE, SHALL BE GATHERED TOGETHER IN A NEW HEAVEN AND NEW EARTH WITH A NEW JERUSALEM. THEN TRULY, O LORD, WILL THERE BE "PEACE ON EARTH AND GOODWILL TOWARD MEN."

BE GRACIOUS TO US AND GIVE US STRENGTH. BLESSED ART THOU, O LORD OUR GOD, RULER OF THE UNIVERSE. WE THANK YOU FOR SUSTAINING US ALL TO THIS DAY.

BLESSED BE THE LORD. IT IS IN THE NAME OF YESHUA HA MESHACH THAT WE ASK THESE THINGS. AMEN.

SPOTLIGHT ON NARRATOR AND PRIESTLY FIGURE

NARRATOR: The Seder traditionally ends with everyone saying: "Next year in Jerusalem!" However, the Christian Jew and Gentile look past this earth and time and toward the New Jerusalem, the moment when as the Apostle John said in Revelation 21, [1] "Then I saw a new heaven and a new earth; for the first heaven and the first earth passed away, and there is no longer any sea. [2] And I saw the holy city, new Jerusalem, coming down out of heaven from God, made ready as a bride adorned for her husband." That is the day, the day of the New Jerusalem to which, all of us look.

PRIESTLY FIGURE: *And everyone said:*

ALL: Next year in the New Jerusalem!

SPOTLIGHT ONLY ON NARRATOR

NARRATOR: And so – according to the ancient customs, statutes, and law – ends the Passover Seder.

[Shofar blows.]

[In prayer]

May the good **LORD** go with you and be with all of you and your loved ones, carrying you safely home and blessing you in the year to come.

[Recorded Postlude–1 hour or until cleanup is complete]

END

Standard sized copies of the Passover Script and a Haggadah may be ordered from:

BAC Publishing
14450 Old Galveston Road
Webster, Texas 77598
(281) 480-5683

APPENDIX B.
Passover Checklists

The following checklists are provided as a general guide to help you conduct your Passover, whether in a small or a large group setting. I would strongly encourage you to start with the guidelines furnished and then adapt them for your own specific needs.

Following a Passover, you will have become so absorbed in "what to do" that you will think, "I don't need any guidelines. I've got it, now. I won't forget!" HINT: You will. Develop, keep and then use and reuse your guiding checklists. They will save you considerable time in reinventing the wheel.

- A BASIC PASSOVER CHECKLIST
- DO'S AND DON'TS FOR PASSOVER
- PASSOVER COMMITTEES - *Roles and Responsibilities*
- PROGRAM COMMITTEE CHECKLIST
- MUSIC COMMITTEE CHECKLISTS
- PUBLICITY COMMITTEE CHECKLIST
- FOOD COMMITTEE CHECKLIST
- TABLE FOOD AND ITEM CHECKLIST
- UNIQUE ITEMS REQUIRED FOR PASSOVER

A BASIC PASSOVER CHECKLIST

☐ Tablecloth and napkins: It is customary to dress up the Seder table with an elegant tablecloth and cloth napkins.

☐ Candles on the table and throughout a room provide a warm glow. A small table menorah is also an elegant touch. Remember to get correct ones (7 not 9 candles). Place something under the menorah and candles to catch any drips. You'll be glad you did.

☐ Dishes and utensils: Whether you choose formal china or everyday dishware, keep it nice for the service

☐ Glassware: Two glasses are needed for each place setting, one for water and one for wine.

☐ An extra wine goblet: One additional wine glass is placed in the center of the table for Elijah, the prophet (who attendees hope will visit each Seder dinner to foretell the arrival of the Messiah). For a group Seder, the wine glass may be at the host or leader's table.

☐ Food and beverages: Quantity dependent upon number attending.

☐ Seder Plate: Prepare the Seder Plate to contain the foods that are symbolic of the Exodus story.

☐ Saltwater: Each attendee is given a small dish of salt water in which they may dip their "greens" during the service.

☐ Additional plates of karpas, charoset, and maror: To make things more convenient for guests, you can also set small dishes containing each item next to every place setting.

☐ Matzah: Each table should contain three pieces of matzah on a plate, covered with a cloth or napkin, and set near the table's Seder Plate.

☐ Wine or Kosher grape Juice: Ensure that there is enough wine or Kosher grape juice on the table so that each guest may have four glasses as called for in the Seder.

Miscellaneous

☐ Copies of the Haggadah: One copy of the Haggadah is placed on top of each guest's plate or under the napkin.

☐ Basin and towel: A small basin filled with warm water and a towel is placed on or near the table for the hand-washing rituals that occur during the service.

☐ Pillows: It's traditional, though not essential, for each guest to recline on a pillow during the ceremony to symbolize the comfort of freedom.

DO'S AND DON'TS FOR PASSOVER

DO leave yourself enough time to send invitations and get responses.

DO leave enough time to clean, prepare and arrange the Passover Table to look as beautiful as possible.

DO consider placing a plastic cloth under the cups to catch the drippings of the wine or Kosher grape juice. Come laundry or dry cleaning day, you will be glad you did. If you are using wine, consider using Israeli wines.

DO remember to hide the Afikomen before the service, whether at home or in the church. At the appropriate time in the Seder, you will offer a reward to the child that finds it (you might have to guide them a bit if their discovery modules are off).

DO use as attractive a set of dishes and flatware as you can. They need not be fancy but should represent your "family's best" in honor of the occasion.

DO consider occasionally purchasing a few unique items such as an Elijah cup, a Passover Plate or unique bowls and towels for the washing. These might become keepsakes, and you would want to later pass them on to your loved ones.

DO have uniform *Haggadot* (plural form of *Haggadah*) that are reliable and easily read and understood.

DO plan for the traditional hymns that may appear in your service. If you have selected performers, do rehearse their entrances and their timing.

DON'T forget to obtain the Afikomen gift early.

DON'T neglect preparing a Leader's Guide that becomes an essential interface between the Passover guests and the Seder service.

DON'T forget to rehearse as many parts of the Passover as possible before the event. Rehearsal makes the Leader shine and the Young Child asking the four questions sparkle. It's also a good idea to rehearse the Honored Wife's lighting of the candles.

DON'T rush the Seder service; it is a time meant for learning and reflection. Take time to be sure that the critical points are understood.

Passover Committees
Roles and Responsibilities

Introduction

Orchestrating the Passover is like running any large event; thus, many committees must work together and independently for a smooth-running event. Committee chairs must meet periodically to assure that all functions are understood and completed. One final meeting approximately one-week prior, and several meetings the week of Passover, may be necessary. Those involved in the set-up and the program may want to dedicate several days the week of the event to assure that everything has been done.

The Director should appoint or seek volunteers as chairs for each committee and then set up periodic status meetings (or check with each chair individually).

Roles and Responsibilities

Producer: The Producer is responsible for the event and coordinates the activities among the Director, the committees and the church. He/she maintains the financial coordination and accountability for the Passover Seder.

Director: The Director is responsible for supervising and coordinating the overall event, rehearsals, and committees, as well as for the selection and direction of the event's writing, staging, and performance.

1. Interfaces with the church management to set a date and time for the Passover and reserve the building for rehearsals.
2. Appoints or asks volunteers to fill committee chair positions *(committee chairs should recruit their own teams).*
3. Sends out general informational notes.
4. Schedules periodic committee meetings, including a final status meeting one-week prior.
5. Sets the rehearsal dates and informs the committee chairs.

Committee Chairs

The committee chairs are responsible for and see that all the items in the check sheets (attachments to this document) have been completed and to coordinate with other committees to make sure there are no "holes" in the production.

1. Attend meetings called by the Passover Producer and/or Director.
2. Recruit committee members that they need.
3. Follow through to make sure that all tasks included in the check sheets are done.
4. Ask for help from the Passover's Producer or Director if help is needed.

Organization

The attachments to this document contain check sheets for each committee. The "how to" is left to each committee.

1. Program Committee

The Program Committee is responsible for the Haggadah (printing and updating), the program notebooks used by the cast, drafting and printing the program, recruiting the cast, and rehearsals. The Program Committee interfaces with the Music Committee and the Committees responsible for the Passover Performance.

2. Music Committee

The Music Committee is responsible for all music and sound CDs necessary to support the program. The Music Committee selects the songs, recruits the singers, sets rehearsals for the singers, provides/recruits musicians or recorded background music and rehearsal tapes and keeps/catalogs all hard copy music and CDs for future years. The Music Committee also drafts and rehearses the child for the four questions, the honored wife, and shofar player. The Music Committee interfaces with the Program Committee and other performance committees as needed.

3. Publicity Committee

The Publicity Committee handles printing tickets, selling tickets, designing fliers, putting the information in the appropriate church and community newsletters (or other suitable electronic distribution), turning the checks/cash to the church (or depositing), and providing a status/final report for sales and money. Typically, the church will reimburse those who have bought items to use for Passover. During ticket sales, the committee should determine the number of children who will be needing childcare and recruit three people for nursery duty. The Publicity Committee interfaces with the Director and the other Committees to report the number of attendees.

4. Food Committee

The Food Committee assures that all the food is bought, prepared, served, and cleaned up. The Food Committee chooses the menu that includes lamb and other appropriate Jewish sides, including dessert and drinks. The food also consists of the unique items that are included in the Seder Plate, the grape juice for the "cups of wine" during the program, the Charoses, the unleavened bread, and all associated paper goods, as well as the candles. The Food Committee interfaces with the Set-up/Clean-up Committee to coordinate where the food service tables are located, as well as times to set out the Seder Plates, drinks, and food before and during the Passover event. The Food Committee disposes of leftover food, and the Clean-up Committee then takes over with a final cleaning of the dishes/facilities.

5. Staging Committee

The Staging Committee sets up, takes down, and puts away the "props" for the Passover (similar to a Stage committee for a play). The Staging Committee sets up the "stage," lights, sound, and any large-ticket items for "ambiance" as requested by the Director. Costuming is a subset of this committee. If a live lamb is involved, this committee will oversee obtaining and setting this as well. This does not include the tables (as this is done by the Set-up/Clean-up Committee). The Staging Committee interfaces with the Director.

6. Set-up / Clean-up Committee

The Set-up and Clean-up Committees are responsible for the primary table and chair layout to accommodate the food serving and the guest seating arrangements. This includes recruiting help to do the intensive labor well ahead of time. Tables should be set up as far in advance as possible but not so soon that it interferes with other church activities. The committee must assure that they know where all items came from to return them to their proper place for next year. Set-up includes tablecloths, table items (washbasins, pitchers, menorahs, candles, filled Seder Plates, and filled water glasses and pitchers. The Set-up Committee assures that enough help is present to carry the prepared food to the tables during the first half of the Passover presentation. This committee interfaces with the Food Committee and the other committees as needed

7. Childcare Committee

The Childcare committee is responsible for the care of the children who attend the Passover celebration. This includes creating a hands-on program to educate and entertain the children on the basics of the Passover. They will recruit teachers and helpers to present the program to the children too young to participate with the adults. They are also responsible for creating and printing a Passover activity booklet for the children who will be attending with their parents.

8. Management Committee

This is a small committee of two or three, who oversees the horizontal and vertical integration of all activities. This committee interfaces with all committee chairs and the Director.

Program Committee Checklist

Coordinate with the church to approve and schedule the date and time of Passover Seder.

1. Schedule a **Kickoff Meeting** and send out an announcement

2. Recruit committee chairs

3. Conduct initial Kickoff Meeting.

At Kickoff Meeting

- Schedule at least two interim meetings

- Set a date for final "week before" meeting

- Set dates for initial program run-through

- Set dates for "week-of" rehearsals

- Name committee chairs and recruit volunteers.

- Establish the price of tickets

4. Coordinate with the church calendar to reserve the location for the Passover and rehearsal dates.

5. Print new tickets

6. Update and print Program Book with previous year's notes and those from the Initial run-through.

7. Update Haggadot and arrange for printing

8. Update and print program.

Music Committee Checklists

1. Make recommendation to Director for songs for the year.

2. Inventory music and CDs, etc., from a previous year.

3. Recruit singers/musicians for each song.

4. Recruit triangle player for use during the Passover discussion of the plagues that struck the Egyptians.

5. Provide demo/background CD and music/words for each song in an individual package.

6. Recruit child for four questions and provide his part.

7. Recruit mother (coordinate with Director).

8. Recruit musician(s) for congregational song/worship band.

9. Coordinate with sound folks to create a CD with music.

10. Participate in initial run-through to verify song cues.

11. Verify that Director updates Program Book with new music, lighting, sound cues for all.

12. Schedule rehearsals for singers, including final dress rehearsal (coordinate with Director).

13. Verify prelude, music during the meal, and postlude tapes.

14. Double check sound effects like a shofar and "children with Elijah."

15. Make sure to have a CD-to-CD recorder (or other appropriate electronic recording media).

16. During Passover—work with Sound Committee to cue singers.

17. Have a place for the music performers to sit if they do not have tickets

18. Post-Passover—collect, organize, and store all music and Passover-specific items.

Publicity Committee Checklist

1. Set up an Excel spreadsheet with columns for Ticket #, Paid, Name, and Notes (childcare).

2. Coordinate with BACC to be in the Information Booth starting at 6 weeks out to sell tickets.

3. Draft initial and follow-on notice to put into bulletin and newsletter.

4. Notify area churches and old BACC friends.

5. Determine what promotional efforts are to be undertaken such as paid advertising with radio/newspapers (friend-to-friend and person to person word of mouth seem to yield more better results).

6. Turn over checks/cash to church on a weekly basis and tally ticket sales.

7. Provide a report to all so adequate planning can occur.

8. Work with Director for church announcements, Power Point shows, etc. Do not surprise the ministers. Plan for review and approval and scheduling of special reports if needed.

9. Provide the Director with "comp" tickets for ministerial staff (including Children's Director). Consider also for secretarial staff.

10. Provide a final report.

Food Committee Checklist

The Food Committee may have several groups within it to assign and carry out the following tasks.

Required Meal and Paper Goods:

Each table needs "dressing." The numbers of plates, drinking vessels, and eating utensils depend upon the number of place settings at each table. Each setting should have a beverage glass, a wine glass, an eating plate (glass, china or disposable), eating utensils and the like.

Each table should be furnished with one Seder Plate, a pitcher of wine (kosher grape juice) for the pouring and one small table menorah (7 candles). A large plastic bowl and small towels are needed for washing. Each place setting should have enough Haggadah copies for each attendee and of course a copy of the evening's program.

Table Food and Item Checklist

1. Develop an estimate as to the number of attendees anticipated. Experience has demonstrated that whatever size facility is available, that facility will be filled.

2. Determine the amount of lamb needed and order

3. Order other meats if desired. (Note: pork should be excluded, but fish, chicken or fowl may be served.)

4. Select appropriate side dishes and determine the amount to be prepared.

5. 5.   Select appropriate desserts and determine amount to be prepared.

6. Select the type of beverage and assess quantity needed. For cost purposes, water, tea, etc., are recommended.

7. Determine the number of and type of wine glasses to be used. Recommend plastic ones for cost savings as well as for appearance.

8. Select the beverage glasses to be used. Recommend plastic for cost savings and cleanup purposes. Certain quality plastic dishes, if not heated, can be cleaned and reused.

9. Select the total number of Seder Plates needed (one per table). Unless there is a substantial organizational budget that can afford authentic Passover Plates, a "lookalike" foil or plastic plate (as illustrated on the previous page) is recommended. Plates with six divisions plus a center space are easily found at local stores or online.

10. Determine and select the appropriate quantity of the following eating utensils:
    - Dessert forks
    - Dinner napkins
    - Two-ounce clear ramekins with lids for saltwater
    - Dessert napkins

- Top-quality disposable silverware

11. Determine the amount of and purchase coffee or tea

12. Determine the amount of and purchase Pam (for spraying menorahs to help limit candle-drip cleaning problems)

13. Determine the number of and purchase table doilies for the table matzah

14. Determine the number of candles needed for the on-table menorahs. There will be *seven* candles per menorah. (Caution: don't make the mistake of acquiring Hanukah menorahs with nine candles.

15. Candles or oil lamps for tables (check to see what is left from the previous year). Two or three large candles are usually needed per table. It is the combination of candles that furnish the "table" lighting. This strongly influences and improves the look and mood of the dinner.

16. Ice required either from the organization's ice machine or from purchase.

Unique Items Required for Passover

There are some "unique items" required for the Passover service. The quantity depends upon the number attending and/or the number of dining tables that are set up.

- **Charoset or Haroseth**: The "charoset" or "clay" of apples, nuts, cinnamon, and wine represents the bricks and mortar the Israelites were forced to make under Pharaoh's taskmasters (see recipes). Approximately one gallon per hundred guests.

- **Bitter Herbs or Maror (two)** symbolizing the bitterness of slavery in Egypt. It is made of (1) grated horseradish or whole horseradish root, Maror consists of grated horseradish or whole horseradish root with (2) romaine lettuce. Approximately four ounces are needed per six place settings.

- **Salt** for the small saltwater containers on each table.

- **Matzah** is an unleavened flatbread made from flour and water. The bread may be made or purchased. Quantity depends upon the number of attendees.

- **Kosher grape juice or wine:** There is a traditional requirement that four cups of wine (or juice) are to be consumed during the Passover meal. This applies to both men and women.

- **A mustard seed:** Used in place of the Babylonian egg. It serves as a reminder of faith as Christ reminded us in **Luke 17:6:** *And the Lord said, "If you had faith like a mustard seed, you would say to this mulberry tree, 'Be uprooted and be planted in the sea,' and it would obey you."*

Checklist for Servers (Wait-Staff)

1. Recommend that the organization recruit its evening dinner's wait-staff from the organization's high school and college members who may be fundraising for missions and camp activities. This can be paid for from the per-ticket sold. It can also be a secondary fundraiser.

2. Recruit one wait-staff per four tables to refill drinks, explain the order of service, tell where bathrooms are located, transparent plates, clear serving containers, discuss eating condiments (It's OK to eat Charoset and drink grape juice during the meal).

3. Attire wait-staff in costume (it can be of the period or simple such as white shirts and dark slacks). Check with Staging for coordination.

4. After Program begins, wait-staff helps chef move food from the kitchen to serving tables, if necessary.

5. Wait-staff fills glasses with water when the table leaves to get their food, or if served at the table, as it is served.

6. Wait-staff removes washing bowl, small Seder Plates, and salt water at the break for dinner.

7. Wait-staff clears plates after the food has been eaten. Scrape plates and stack to reduce the amount of garbage.

8. Collect names of wait-staff for acknowledgment in the Seder program.

Staging Committee Setup Checklists

Staging checklists for the week of the Seder

A. **Two days before:**

1. Wash all bowls and pitchers and white towels for washing hands.

2. Locate tablecloths; press and iron if necessary.

3. Set up tables

4. Spread tablecloths on tables.

5. Cut small 10-inch square plastic cloth, which is placed atop the center table doily on which the menorah sits. The plastic catches much of the candle drippings, saving the tablecloth and doily.

6. Clean menorahs with Brasso (assuming they are made of brass).

7. Spray menorahs with Pam cooking spray (to protect against drippings)

8. Mix one pound of salt with one gallon of water, stir and pour into the small plastic ramekins on each table. Add cover.

9. Acquire chafing dishes as needed to keep the food warm.

B. **One day before-**

1. Place all paper goods on the tables (already with tablecloths). When everything is on the table, arrange according to the placement graphic appearing in Chapter 8.

   a. Clear plastic water glasses, according to seating. Leave stacked in a corner of the table to facilitate smooth ice and water filling before the program.

   b. Clear plastic wine glasses.

   c. Clear plastic forks, spoons and knives

   d. Small clear ramekins with saltwater dip

   e. Napkins

   f. One menorah in the center on top of the plastic square

   g. Seven candles for the menorah,

   h. One small box of matches, 1 long match (Home Depot)

i. One muslin Afikomen bag placed on the bread tray

j. Salt & pepper

k. Nine Haggadot (the order of service manual)

l. One 10-inch clear plastic square for under the doily

m. One purple runner, placed crossways in the middle of the table

n. One white 10-inch square doily for under the menorah

o. Two clear-glass globe-style candleholders

p. Two small oil lamps to put into glass globe-style candle holders - Pull wick out 1/4"-1/2" for a brighter flame. Light to see,

2. **Arrange the table according to the diagram:**

a. 10-inch square white doily on top of "10-inch square" clear-plastic in the center of the table

b. Menorah on top of the doily

c. Seven Candles for each table's menorah (use a menorah, not the special one used for Hanukkah).

d. Each of nine place settings has flatware with a wine glass and a water glass above the knife and spoon

e. Small, clear, covered ramekin of saltwater to the right of the spoon

f. Place oil lamps in glass globes. Place on either side of the menorah.

g. Set up the *head-table* on raised platform/stage area.

3 **Set the place settings; flatware, wine glass, water glass, napkin as well as—**

a. Matzah bag (small linen bag which holds the matzah at the table)

b. Special Passover for the stage-table (Priestly Figure and family)

c. Table Menorah (7 candles)

d. The Haggadah

C. Seder Day Set up

1. Morning of Seder, 8 a.m.

a. Recommend setting the thermostat to 60 degrees. (AC can be reset later. The room will warm up as bodies enter and are seated.)

b. Set up the buffet service (the easiest way to serve).

c. Set up the tables needed for each of two buffet lines.

d. Place chafing dishes/food on each buffet line.

g. Place Sterno cans for warming food if needed and matches on each buffet line.

h. Place sufficient serving utensils on each buffet line.

i. Place plates on the starting end of buffet lines (for attendees)

J. Prepare tent labels for the food. Remember, some foods will be new to the attendees.

2. Set up of dessert tables

a. Set tables for two (or more if needed) separate dessert areas.

b. Prepare tent labels to identify desserts.

c. Set out dessert plates for attendees.

3. 1 ½ hours before Seder. Prepare Seder Plate and Seder Table

a. One pitcher of ice water

b. One pitcher half full of grape juice (if grape juice is used instead of wine)

c. Fill one special Seder Plate for each table

    1) 1/3 bunch of parsley, cleaned and broken into smaller pieces

    2) ½ cup of charoset in one section

    3) One shank bone

    4) Two oz. horseradish, in one section

4. One hour before Seder, wait-staff is costumed. Afterward, at each table, do the following:

1. Add one aluminum filled Seder Plate from the kitchen

2. Fill glasses with ice and water.

3. Place three-matzah bread in matzah bag (called the matzo tosh).

4. Set out four platters of dessert on each table: fruit, macaroons, yellow cake, and nut cake

D. Servers' "To-Do List" on Day of Passover.

1. Wait-staff should arrive at 6:00 p.m. One wait-staff per table recommended, but no less that one per three tables.

2. Fill glasses with ice and water.

3. Light the candles fifteen minutes before the program start.

4. Be available to greet and usher in guests. Point out restrooms to non-BACC participants. Be open to explain how to use the Haggadah and to describe the order of service, when dinner is served, when to eat the condiments, and the time to drink the grape juice. If the attendee is a newcomer – he or she will think the grape juice is part of the served refreshments.

5. When the tables are dismissed to the buffet lines, fill glasses with water; remove the washing bowl, white towel with blue stripe, and salt water for dipping

6. Bring washing bowls to the kitchen cleaning area. Place the white towel in a basket for future machine washing.

7. When guests get dessert, begin clearing the dinner plates. Empty food scraps in one bucket and stack plates in a trashcan. All wait staff should help each other until everything is cleared away.

8. After dessert dishes are removed, the Seder Plates and salt and pepper shakers are taken to the kitchen area/

9. After the service ends, clear any remaining dishes. Cleaning crew will remove the menorahs and candles and place in the appropriate box.

Clean-up Committee Checklists

Before the Seder

1. Ensure that proper cleaning agents are on-hand such as—
   - Brasso Cleaner for menorahs
   - Liquid Cascade Dishwasher detergent for spot-cleaning tablecloths after Seder

2. Set out for the crew the appropriate checklists that you feel are needed. This would include directions for what to clean, where things are stored, put away or set aside for return to the owner.

After the Seder

1. Post Time of Arrival: For example, it might be that Clean-up Crew #1 arrives at 7:30 to begin. Clean-up efforts will be ongoing in all food preparation areas (kitchen, etc.)

2. Caution the Clean-up crews to take special care not to cause unnecessary noise or disturbances during the service.

3. Wash, dry, and put away all food preparation dishes that remain in the cooking areas.

4. Rinse and stack discarded pans (not necessary to scrub). Afterward, the final stack will be put into the garbage and discarded or recycled.

5. Wash, dry, and place back into the storage boxes all of the water bowls, wine (juice) pitchers, and Seder Plates.

6. Return plastic ware in boxes back to the storage areas.

7. At 1½ hours after the start of the service, prepare 3 (or more if needed) large pots of boiling water to clean the menorahs and clean the shank bones.

8. Designate a laundry person/persons to take home tablecloths and white hand towels.

9. Return chairs and table to their assigned storage places.

10. The lamb shank bones from the Seder Plates can be cleaned, stored and reused.
    a. Boil shank bones for 15 minutes.
    b. Drain and wrap in dry dishtowels until cool and very dry.

   c. Wrap the bones in paper towels and place in one or two gallon-size Ziploc bags. They need to be double-wrapped to absorb moisture and cushion the sharp edges. If they are boiled and not dried thoroughly, they will mildew and need to be replaced the following year.

12. Remove all trash to appropriate bags and containers.

13. Service all tables as required:

   a. Wax removal: Collect menorahs and take to the kitchen area for cleaning.

   b. Throw out old candles, making sure they are completely cool before removing.

   c. Collect plastic pitchers and remove to be laundered.

   d. Return baskets to boxes that go upstairs to Passover storage.

   e. Tables – collect any table Items that are not to be washed.

   f. Use a rolling cart to collect salt and pepper shakers,. Return to their boxes.

   g. Use a rolling cart to collect oil burners (blow them out), straw baskets, and Afikomen bags. These should be placed in their proper containers.

   h. Tablecloths: Once items are off the tables, spot treat all spots with Liquid Cascade.

   i. If there are not two bottles of the Liquid Cascade, have one cleanup person put some Liquid Cascade in a bowl and blot on the spots.

   j. Remove and fold tablecloths and remove to be laundered.

   k. Wash tables.

   l. Return tables to their proper storage area.

   m. Floors

     1) Mop all of the floors where needed.

   n. If any wall hangings such as curtains, etc., have been used, then take them down and put them away.

Childcare Committee Checklist

1. Coordinate with the ticket sellers how many children's tickets are sold and how many children need childcare.

2. Decide on the price of the child's meal ticket.

3. Create a hands-on children's program that includes explaining the Passover story and its symbols, the Seder Plate and its elements. The program should provide the opportunity to eat the charoset and matzah bread, acting out parts of the Passover story, an object lesson, and a craft.

4. Create and print a children's activity booklet. This will be given to the child participating in the adult program as well as those in childcare.

5. Decide on the menu for the children and the place where it will be served to them.

6. If possible, children's teachers and childcare workers should be recruited from the church's college and high school members who are raising funds for mission projects.

7. Recruit two teachers to prepare and present the children's program. They will wear costumes during their story-telling time. The teachers can be childcare workers.

8. Recruit two childcare workers for every eight children.

9. Collect children's data for parent's names, food allergy information, and parents' table number.

10. The childcare workers will assist the children during the craft and mealtime activities.

11. The childcare workers will supervise the youngsters during their story times and play time.

12. Childcare workers will serve the children a meal. This can be from the buffet table or a separate menu.

13. Childcare workers will clear the meal served to children.

14. Workers are responsible for returning all toys to proper places and return tables and chairs to their appropriate place.

15. This committee will interface with the Program committee for the activity booklet, the Publicity committee for the childcare numbers and the Staging committee for the costumes.

APPENDIX B – Passover Checklists

About the Author

Dr. Warren Chaney is an American author, filmmaker, behavioral scientist, and a pioneer in early television. He holds a Doctorate *(Ph.D.* in *Behavioral Science* and Management), an MBA *(Finance),* and a *Bachelor of Science* with a double major *(Marketing and Speech and Theatre).*

During a wide-ranging career, Dr. Chaney as of the date of printing, written twenty-eight books, sixteen screenplays, ten theatrical dramas, and over 400 professional and non-professional magazine and journal articles. He has written entries for *Colliers Encyclopedia* and was an editor for two publications, one in health care and a fictional detective magazine. Dr. Chaney has produced nine feature films and directed eight in addition to producing and directing numerous television productions including 150 episodes of the pioneering television series, *Magic Mansion.* He has received considerable recognition and awards for his film and television work.

Dr. Chaney has a substantial background in behavioral science and management consulting. His former clients included such notables as NASA, Bell Telephone, Hoffman LA Roche, Celanese Chemical Corporation, the U.S. House and Senate Labor Management Sub-Committee, Humana Corporation, St. Joseph Hospitals, and many others. He has been featured in national publications and mass media to include *Good Morning America, Real People, PM Magazine, CBS Weekend News and ABC Radio.*

Chaney established the first public university *Health Services Administration* program for the state of Texas. He has served on various boards of directors and advisory boards of public companies. He was an officer in the *United States Army* and served in multiple military commands during the *Vietnam Era.* He was born in Kentucky, a native of Hopkinsville, and educated in Tennessee and Texas.

Dr. Chaney now resides in Houston, Texas, is married and has five children.

Lightning Source UK Ltd.
Milton Keynes UK
UKHW022136100521
383500UK00003B/318